D0957841

The 101 HABITS

of highly successful

NOVELISTS

Insider Secrets from Top Writers

Andrew McAleer

adamsmedia

Avon, Massachusetts

To my daughter, Trinity McAleer
An altar, not a station

And to my dear friend, Robin Moore
A Boston Brahmin adventurer

Copyright © 2008 by Andrew McAleer
All rights reserved.
This book, or parts thereof, may not be reproduced in any
form without permission from the publisher; exceptions are
made for brief excerpts used in published reviews.

Published by
Adams Media, a division of F+W Media, Inc.
57 Littlefield Street, Avon, MA 02322. U.S.A.
www.adamsmedia.com

ISBN 10: 1-59869-589-4
ISBN 13: 978-1-59869-589-2

Printed in the United States of America.

J I H G F E D C B

Library of Congress Cataloging-in-Publication Data
is available from the publisher.

This publication is designed to provide accurate and authoritative information
with regard to the subject matter covered. It is sold with the understanding that
the publisher is not engaged in rendering legal, accounting, or other professional
advice. If legal advice or other expert assistance is required, the services of a com-
petent professional person should be sought.
  —From a *Declaration of Principles* jointly adopted by a Committee of the
American Bar Association and a Committee of Publishers and Associations

Many of the designations used by manufacturers and sellers to distinguish their
product are claimed as trademarks. Where those designations appear in this book
and Adams Media was aware of a trademark claim, the designations have been
printed with initial capital letters.

This book is available at quantity discounts for bulk purchases.
For information, please call 1-800-289-0963.

CONTENTS

Part II: CREATIVITY / 31

Part III: **DISCIPLINE / 93**

Chapter 6: The Writing Habit 95

Chapter 7: The Challenges 106

Chapter 8: The Editing Process 129

Part IV: **THE BUSINESS / 153**

Chapter 9: Networks. 155

Chapter 10: The Publishing Business 180

Chapter 11: Your Readers 199

Chapter 12: The Future 205

FOREWORD
BY BILL PRONZINI

Professional writers are a highly diverse group. Not only do we produce many different types of novels, we tend to view the craft of fiction writing in a manner as individualistic as our subject matter, styles, and visions. Put a large group of us together in a room and call for a general theoretical discussion of what makes a successful novel and a successful career, and you're certain to have disparate opinions and more than one heated argument.

Yet when it comes to analyzing the nuts-and-bolts specifics of writing and selling as a guide for the beginner, our views and advice are remarkably similar. This is because professional writers are practical to a fault; the one principle we all agree on is the necessity to create the very best novels of which we're capable in order to realize the optimum financial and critical benefits. Literary theory and philosophy are excellent fodder for conversation and argument, but they're not what professional writing is fundamentally about. Nor are they what *The 101 Habits of Highly Successful Novelists* is about. The purpose of this book is to help you do what we do: write the best novel of which you're capable, experience the pleasure and satisfaction of seeing it published, and then reap the rewards. In short, it's a straightforward, no nonsense, professional approach to fiction writing.

Andrew McAleer has done an outstanding job of organizing the material here into chapters that combine the instructive words of novelists past and present with his own expert commentary. Every aspect is covered: important general topics such as being creative and original, the art of natural storytelling, commitment to success, setting realistic goals and high standards of excellence; detailed how-tos and don't-dos of plot construction, characterization, dialogue, conflict, and other story elements; tips on marketing, finding an agent, utilizing promotional options, and networking; even counsel on how to deal with such drawbacks as rejection, criticism, and fear of failure.

Read the individual quotes carefully, not only for their practical advice but for the insights they give into the men and women who wrote them. For this is how successful novelists think. Understanding the professional mindset can help you adopt a similar perspective toward your own work.

In a sense, reading this book is like being invited into the roomful of established storytellers, being given the opportunity to sit down with each of us and get to know us while we discuss the various tricks of our trade. There are no better teachers, after all, than the voices of experience.

As practical and invaluable as *The 101 Habits of Highly Successful Novelists* is, you should keep in mind that it does not contain a magical formula for becoming a published writer. There is no such formula, nor are there any shortcuts to success. The instruction offered here is strictly utilitarian, remember; it must be studied, taken to heart, and then adapted and incorporated into your own work and work ethic. The key to success lies with dedication, perseverance, and—the ultimate goal of pros as well as beginners—the consistent desire to become a better writer tomorrow than today.

Good luck!

INTRODUCTION

Everything nourishes what is strong already.—Jane Austen

When I first set out to write *The 101 Habits of Highly Successful Novelists*, I had one goal in mind: to help aspiring novelists achieve their dreams of publishing novels. I believe firmly—thanks to the generous contributions of some of the best and most experienced novelists of our time—that my goal has been brought to bountiful fruition.

What you have hitched your wagon to here is more than a book. It is a bumper crop of literary harvest propagated from the arduous toil of the contributors. You have at your fingertips the advice and wisdom of novelists who have successfully dug in and made fourteen-carat hay out of this business, some for more than half a century. This book is filled with advice from the most successful novelists from the most successful genres—romance, crime and suspense, Westerns, science fiction, and fantasy—such as Mary Higgins Clark, Elmore Leonard, Robin Moore, and Lawrence Block.

I'm not going to take much credit for this work because it wasn't written per se. It was germinated, and I just tilled the soil a little bit. This book was sown from the struggles, perseverance, and triumphs of its contributors, who simply would not quit when critics told them it couldn't be done, that they were wasting their time, that they shouldn't quit their day jobs, that writing was too tough, and that dreams are a waste of time. These novelists would have none of it, and you are the benefactor of the fruits of their labor.

The contributors to this book have brought a burgeoning cornucopia to the table. It's a crop consisting of nourishing words on how these indefatigable artists write continuously with such success. You can use their experience and advice to cut away the underbrush and prep the soil for planting. Further, you will be able to call on their advice again and again as if they were your helpful neighbors ready to roll up their sleeves and pitch in to help whenever needed.

I hope that this book will become your most trusted writing companion to nurture your muse. And it won't even need watering. Not like those corn plants that the damn rabbits got into.

CONTRIBUTORS

LORI AVOCATO Award-winning and bestselling author of the Pauline Sokol mysteries, including *A Dose of Murder*; *The Stiff and the Dead*; *One Dead Under the Cuckoo's Nest*; *Deep Sea Dead*; *Nip, Tuck, Dead*; and *Dead on Arrival*

BRUCE BALFOUR Author of *Prometheus Road*, *Jack the Ripper*, *The Digital Dead*, and the national bestseller *The Forge of Mars*

MARY BALOGH *New York Times* bestselling historical romantic fiction author of the Bedwyn series, including *Slightly Married*, *Slightly Scandalous*, and *Slightly Wicked* and *Indiscreet*, *Unforgiven*, and *Irresistible*

JILL BARNETT Golden Choice nominee and *New York Times* bestselling historical romance and contemporary novelist of critically acclaimed novels such as *The Days of Summer*, *Wicked*, *Wild*, and *Wonderful*

BEVERLY BARTON *New York Times* bestselling romantic suspense author of the Protectors series, including *Penny Sue Got Lucky*, *Ramirez's Woman*, *Laying His Claim*, and *Keeping Baby Secret*

STEPHANIE KAY BENDEL Author of *Making Crime Pay* and the critically acclaimed romantic thriller *A Scream Away* (written under the pen name Andrea Harris) and *Ellery Queen* contributor

JO BEVERLY Winner of five RITA Awards and two Romantic Times Career Achievement Awards and *New York Times* and *USA Today* bestselling author of more than twenty historical romances, including *Lady Beware*, *The Rogue's Return*, and *To Rescue a Rogue*

JENNIFER BLAKE *New York Times* bestselling author of *Love's Wild Desire*, *Guarded Heart*, and *Rogue's Salute* and recipient of the prestigious Golden Treasure Award for Lifetime Achievement from Romance Writers of America and the Frank Waters Award for Excellence in Fiction

LAWRENCE BLOCK *New York Times* bestselling author; Grand Master of the Mystery Writers of America; and Edgar Allan Poe, Shamus, and Japanese Maltese Falcon Award–winning novelist of the Matthew Scudder, Bernie Rhodenbarr, and Chip Harrison novels, including *Eight Million Ways to Die*, *A Ticket to the Boneyard*, *A Dance at the Slaughterhouse*

JOHNNY D. BOGGS Multi-Spur Award–winning novelist of *Camp Ford* and Western Heritage Wrangler Award–winning novelist of *Spark on the Prairie: The Trial of the Kiowa Chiefs* and writer of other novels, including *The Big Fifty: A Western Story*, *Northfield*, and the Spur-nominated best Western juvenile novel *The Hart Brand*

RHYS BOWEN *Romantic Times* top pick. Agatha, Anthony, and Herodotus Award–winning author of the Constable Evans mysteries and the Molly Murphy mysteries, including *Evans Above*, *Evan Help Us*, *Evanly Bodies*, *Murphy's Law*, and *In Dublin's Fair City*

MICHAEL BRACKEN   Derringer Award–winning author of *Tequila Sunrise*, *All White Girls*, and *Yesterday in Blood and Bone*; vice president of the Private Eye Writers of America; and vice president of the Southwest Chapter Mystery Writers of America

REBECCA BRANDEWYNE   *New York Times*, *Publishers Weekly*, *Los Angeles Times*, and *USA Today* bestselling author of *The Crystal Rose*, *The Ninefold Key*, *The Love Knot*, and *The Outlaw Hearts*. Recipient of the Historical Romance Novelist of the Year Award and the Reviewer's Choice Award for Best Western Romance

PATRICIA BRIGGS   *New York Times* and *USA Today* bestselling author of *On the Prowl*, *Blood Bound*, and *Moon Called*. Author of the Mercedes Thompson series and the Anna and Charles series

SUZANNE BROCKMANN   *New York Times* bestselling author, RITA Award–winning author of the Troubleshooter series about U.S. Navy SEAL Team Sixteen and the Tall, Dark & Dangerous series about SEAL Team Ten, including *Into the Storm*, *Force of Nature*, and *All Through the Night*

JAMES M. CAIN   Grand Master Award winner of the Mystery Writers of America, and author of *The Postman Always Rings Twice*, *Double Indemnity*, *Love's Lovely Counterfeit*, and *Mildred Pierce*

LIZ CARLYLE   *New York Times* bestselling author of the Sins, Lies, and Secrets trilogy and other novels of romance, including *Never Lie to a Lady*, *Never Deceive a Duke*, and *A Woman of Virtue*

CINDA WILLIAMS CHIMA   Skyline Writer's Conference winning author of *The Warrior Heir* (which was also a BookSense Children's Pick in summer 2006) and *The Wizard Heir*

MARY HIGGINS CLARK   Grand Master Award winner of the Mystery Writers of America, past president of the Mystery Writers of America, and worldwide bestselling author of *Where Are the Children?*, *The Cradle Will Fall*, *A Stranger Is Watching*, and *The Christmas Thief* (with Carol Higgins Clark)

BARBARA D'AMATO   Past president of the Mystery Writers of America; past president of Sisters in Crime International; and Mary Higgins Clark, Agatha, and Carl Sandburg Award–winning novelist of *Authorized Personnel Only*, *Death of a Thousand Cuts*, *White Male Infant*, and the Chicago Police series

KIT EHRMAN   Award-winning novelist and Kentucky Literary Award nominee of the Steve Cline mystery series, including critically acclaimed novels such as *At Risk*, *Derby Rotten Scoundrels*, and *Triple Cross*

ED GAFFNEY   Author of the critically acclaimed legal suspense thrillers *Diary of a Serial Killer*, *Premeditated Murder*, *Suffering Fools*, and *Enemy Combatant*

ROBERT GOLDSBOROUGH   Nero Wolfe Award–winning novelist of the Steve "Snap" Malek mystery novels and the Nero Wolfe novels, including *Shadow of the Bomb*, *Three Strikes You're Dead*, *Fade to Black*, and *Murder in E-Minor*

LORI HANDELAND   Romance Writers of America RITA Award-winning and *USA Today* best-selling author of the Night-creature novels, including *Blue Moon, Dark Moon, Midnight Moon,* and *Hidden Moon*

STEPHEN HARRIGAN   *New York Times* bestselling author and Spur, Western Heritage, TCU Texas Award–winning novelist of *Aransas, Jacob's Well, The Gates of the Alamo,* and *Challenger Park*

ELOISA JAMES   *New York Times* bestselling romance author of the Essex Sisters, the Duchess Quartet, and the Pleasures Trilogy series, which include bestsellers *Much Ado About You, Your Wicked Ways,* and *Potent Pleasures*

SABRINA JEFFRIES   *New York Times* bestselling author of the Royal Brotherhood, Swanlea Spinster, and Lord Trilogy series, including bestsellers *Beware a Scots Revenge, Only a Duke Will Do, A Notorious Love,* and *The Pirate Lord*

JOAN JOHNSTON   *New York Times* bestselling author of contemporary and historical romance novels including the Bitter Creek, Captive Heart, and Hawk's Way series, including *The Next Mrs. Blackstone, The Bridegroom,* and *The Temporary Groom*

ELMORE LEONARD   Edgar Allan Poe Award–winning novelist; worldwide bestselling author of *Get Shorty, The Big Bounce, Hombre, Be Cool, Mr. Majestic,* and *The Bounty Hunters*; and past president of the Mystery Writers of America

WILLIAM LINK   Multi Edgar Allan Poe, Ellery Queen, Emmy, Golden Globe, and Peabody Award–winning author; cocreator of *Columbo*, *Mannix*, and the *Cosby Mysteries*; past president of the Mystery Writers of America; coauthor of *Fineman* and *The Playhouse*; and cocreator of the *Murder, She Wrote* television and novel series

JULIA LONDON   *New York Times* and *USA Today* bestselling author of the Thrillseekers Anonymous, Lockhart Family, and Rogues of Regent Street trilogies, including critically acclaimed books such as *The Perils of Pursuing a Prince*, *The School of Heiresses*, *The Secret Lover*, and *Highlander Unbound*

PETER LOVESEY   Crime Writers' Association Golden Dagger, Anthony Award–winning, and bestselling novelist of the Sergeant Cribb and Peter Diamond mystery series, including *Wobble to Death*, *Abracadavar*, *The Last Detective*, *Bloodhounds*, and *Upon a Dark Night*

KAT MARTIN   *New York Times* bestselling historical romance, romantic suspense, and contemporary author of *Scent of Roses*, *The Summit*, and *The Devil's Necklace* and author of the Bride's Necklace Trilogy

JOHN MCALEER   Pulitzer Prize nominated and Edgar Allan Poe and Sherlock Holmes Revere Bowl Award–winning author of the number one bestselling *Unit Pride* and *Coign of Vantage*. Past vice president of the Mystery Writers of America and coauthor of the number one bestselling *Mystery Writing in a Nutshell*

MARY REED MCCALL   Romance Writers of America RITA Award finalist, *Romance Times BOOKreviews* 2006 Best Medieval Romance winner, and bestselling novelist of the Templar Knights Trilogy, *Sinful Pleasures, Beyond Temptation, The Crimson Lady,* and *The Templar's Seduction*

GREGORY MCDONALD   Multi Edgar Allan Poe Award–winning author of the *Fletch* and *Flynn* novels, including *Fletch, Confess Fletch, Fletch Too, Flynn,* and *Flynn's World*; past president of the Mystery Writers of America; and recipient of the Trophees 813 Best Foreign Novel in 1997 for *The Brave*

ROBIN MOORE   *New York Times* number one bestselling author of nearly 100 books, including *The French Connection, The Green Berets, The Happy Hooker,* and *The Khaki Mafia*

JAMES F. MURPHY JR.   Author of *They Were Dreamers: A Saga of the Irish in North America, Quonsett: A Novel of Terror, The Mill,* and *Night Watcher;* professor of English Literature at Boston College; and contributor to *Chicken Soup for the Veteran's Soul*

T.M. MURPHY   Bestselling author of the young adult Belltown Mystery series, including *The Secrets of Belltown, The Secrets of Cranberry Beach, The Secrets of Cain's Castle, The Secrets of Pilgrim Pond,* and *The Secrets of Code Z*

KRIS NERI   Derringer Award winner and Agatha, Anthony, and Macavity–nominated author of the Tracy Eaton Mysteries, including *Revenge of the Gypsy Queen* and *Dem Bones' Revenge* and author of the standalone suspense novel *Never Say Die*

T.J. PERKINS   Award-winning author of the Kim and Kelly mystery series, including *Fantasies Are Murder, The Secret in Phantom Forest, Trade Secret*, and *Image in the Tapestry*, and other critically acclaimed novels such as *The Fire and the Falcon, Wound Too Tight, Mystery of the Attic*, and *On Forbidden Ground*

CARLY PHILLIPS   *New York Times, Publishers Weekly, USA Today*, and Waldenbooks bestselling author of the Ty and Hunter stories, Costas Sisters, Hot Zone, and Simply series, including *Cross My Heart, Summer Lovin', Hot Item*, and *Simply Sexy*

BILL PRONZINI   Grand Master of the Mystery Writers of America, multi Shamus Award–winning and Edgar Allan Poe Award–nominated author of the Nameless Detective series. Mystery, suspense, and Western author of critically acclaimed novels such as *The Stalker, Scattershot, Mourners*, and *Savages*. Past president of the Private Eye Writers of America and recipient of its Lifetime Achievement Award

ROBERT J. RANDISI   Author of the Rat Pack and Texas Hold 'em mystery series and the Gamblers old West series. Author of more than forty novels, including *The Money Gun*; *Luck Be a Lady, Don't Die*; *Everybody Kills Somebody Sometime*; and *The Picasso Flop*. Cofounder of the Private Eye Writers of America

DUSTY RICHARDS   Spur Award–winning novelist of *The Horse Creek Incident* and Oklahoma Writer's Federation Fiction Book of the Year Award–winning novelist of *Abilene Trail, Noble's Way, The Lawless Land*, and *Servant of the Law*

CYNTHIA RIGGS   Sisters in Crime "Most Wanted" author of the Victoria Trumbull mystery series, including *Shooting Star*, *Indian Pipes*, *Jack in the Pulpit*, *The Cranefly Orchid Murders*, and *The Cemetery Yew*

JOANN ROSS   *New York Times* and *USA Today* bestselling author and Romantic Times Career Achievement Award–winning author of *No Safe Place*, *Out of the Storm*, *Confessions*, *Southern Comfort*, the Stewart Sisters and Bad Boys series and the Callahan Brothers Trilogy

S.J. ROZAN   Shamus, Edgar, Nero, Anthony, and Macavity Award–winning novelist of critically acclaimed novels such as *Absent Friends*, *In This Rain*, *A Bitter Feast*, and *China Trade* and president of the Private Eye Writers of America

HANK PHILLIPPI RYAN   *Boston Globe* bestselling author of *Prime Time* and *Face Time*. Edward R. Murrow, Associated Press, and Emmy Award–winning investigative reporter. Board of directors member of Sisters in Crime and the New England chapter of the Mystery Writers of America

R.A. SALVATORE   *New York Times* bestselling author of the Drizzt, the Crimson Shadow, and the Dark Elf Trilogy novels, including *Siege of Darkness*, *The Sword of Bedwyr*, *Homeland*, and *The Orc King*

LINDA SANDIFER   Award-winning author of *The Daughters of Luke McCall* and *Raveled Ends of Sky* (A Women of the West Novel), and *Firelight*. Member of the Western Writers of America

TOM SAWYER   Bestselling novelist of the critically acclaimed mystery/thriller *The Sixteenth Man* and head writer/showrunner of the Emmy Award–winning series, *Murder, She Wrote*

VICKI STIEFEL   Daphne du Maurier Award–winning author of the critically acclaimed Tally Whyte suspense novels, including *Body Parts*, *The Grief Shop*, *The Dead Stone*, and *The Bone Man*

REX STOUT   Past president of the Mystery Writers of America and author of the Nero Wolfe, Dol Bonner, and Tecumseh Fox mystery novels

MILES HOOD SWARTHOUT   Spur Award–winning novelist of *The Sergeant's Lady*; screenwriter of John Wayne's last film, *The Shootist*; and member of the Western Writers of America

WILLIAM G. TAPPLY   Award-winning author of the Brady Coyne and Stoney Calhoun mystery and suspense novels, including *Out Cold*, *Past Tense*, *A Fine Line*, *Scar Tissue*, and *Gray Ghost*; coauthor of *Second Sight* (with Philip R. Craig); and contributing editor for *Field & Stream*

CARRIE VAUGHN   Author of the critically acclaimed werewolf series *Kitty Takes a Holiday*, *Kitty Goes to Washington*, *Kitty and the Midnight Hour*, and *Kitty and the Silver Bullet*

MICHAEL WIECEK   Private Eye Writers of America Shamus Award winner, Derringer Award–winning author of *Exit Strategy*, and director with the New England Chapter of the Mystery Writers of America

Part I

PASSION

My 1955 edition of *The Oxford Universal Dictionary* offers so many definitions for the word "passion" that I almost gave up trying to figure out why the word is so important to the subject of writing.

I found this definition in my travels: "The suffering of pain." I didn't like that one even though it applies all too well to the life of an author. Then there was: "The being affected from without." I have absolutely no idea what that means, but it was a frightening throwback to the college course I took on Analytic Philosophy. Finally, way down deep in a tertiary definition I found: "An aim or object pursued with zeal." Kind of like the Indian arrowhead I bought from the Western Heritage Museum in Oklahoma and gave to my eight-year-old nephew Liam.

Now, it wasn't just any old Indian arrowhead, I informed him that it was a "genuine" Indian arrowhead just as advertised. And I believe it too because I scooped it out from the hundreds that were contained in a genuine wicker basket. Anyway, when I gave it to Liam he inspected it from all angles and came up with question after question about how a Native American bow and arrow actually worked. And being a genuine expert on the subject, I answered each question with a qualified precision P. T. Barnum might have envied. Later, when Liam thought he was alone, I saw him looking at the arrowhead as if it possessed some concealed, magical spirit. Indeed, in Liam's eyes, it did. I could see he wanted to know what was the person like who made it? Its adventures? Who found it and where? In Liam's mind, that little chunk of rock had grand stories to tell. That's passion. And whether he knew it or not, as Liam asked himself these questions and tried to answer them, he was writing.

Perhaps I'm a genuine fool to take on Oxford, but the next time I want to know something about passion, I'll ask the nearest kid.

Chapter 1

A PORTRAIT
OF A NOVELIST

The interest is easy. The concentration . . . you need a very very strong superstructure. . . . You know, you need a big big superstructure and the determination to make it work. Now, one of the big revelations for me, early on as a writer when I was into writing *The Big Nowhere*, was that I realized I could execute whatever I could conceive of.—James Ellroy

$\mathcal{S}$uccessful novelists are not born. They do not have a sixth sense, an extra set of hands, or a third eye. They are dedicated writers—workers really—who start books and don't quit until they are finished, revised, rewritten, and revised some more, again and again and again until their manuscripts are marketable. Successful novelists have families, jobs, and problems. They are individuals bound by the same time constraints as the would-be novelist with "no time" on her hands.

Successful novelists are single mothers, single fathers, lawyers, movie store clerks, reporters, rabbis, steamboat captains, priests, veterans, rabbit trappers, bellhops, etc. Successful novelists are simply people who turn day-to-day grind into literature because they choose to and don't quit when life gets in the way as it always does and always will. And thank God life does get in the way, otherwise they would have nothing to write about.

1. Being Creative and Original

The man who has no imagination has no wings.—Muhammad Ali

Your novel is what *your* thoughts make it. Your life is unique and like no other. There will never be another one of you. Your singular experiences help make you who you are and what you are about. Inside of you are your unique novel, characters, and story line. Only you can create the novel you wish to create. No one else can do it but you. I have edited a small award-winning magazine for the past decade and have read thousands of short story submissions and the cover letters that accompany them. I cringe when I read "My story is just like . . ." or "My characters are reminiscent of . . ." I ask myself: What is *your* story? Who are *your* characters? And believe me, other editors and agents ask these same questions. Readers want, indeed demand, and are entitled to originality. They want to explore the new world you have created and to meet the original and exciting people who exist in your mind and not in some other writer's work.

Now, let's look into the minds of these creative authors who have brought us so many wonderful new worlds and different characters.

> **GREGORY MCDONALD**   People ask me how to write a book. That's the wrong question. The question ought to be, how does one write *this* book? I don't know. Only the person who conceives of a book, short story, poem, painting, or piece of music really has the ability to bear it and birth it . . . fulfill it, in accordance with itself.

> **BILL PRONZINI** Always do your own work. Never try to imitate favorite or bestselling authors. Never follow current trends; what is a hot topic today may well be ice cold by the time a novel is written and submitted for publication. Imitators are seldom successful. An individual's unique style and vision are what editors are looking for.

> **PETER LOVESEY** Beware of the cliché. By this I mean not only the cliché phrase ("It's an old trick, major, but it might just work."), but the cliché plot (the murderer turns out to be the narrator) and the cliché style. Don't try to be a second Raymond Chandler or J.K. Rowling. By all means learn from successful writers, but be yourself, and say it freshly.

> **CARRIE VAUGHN** Don't compare yourself to others. There will always be someone who writes faster, or slower, or gets a bigger advance, or better advertising. Everyone's career and writing process is a little different. Follow your own path.

2. Being a Natural Storyteller

The art of art, the glory of expression, and the sunshine of the light of letters, is simplicity.—Walt Whitman

Baseball enthusiasts often contend that Ted Williams was a natural hitter. While there may be some truth to this, what *is* certain, is that Ted Williams *loved* to hit a baseball. He would talk about the science of hitting a baseball constantly, and he even wrote a book on the subject. Williams would also visit lumberyards to personally select the wood used to mill his baseball bats.

Likewise, the natural storyteller requires more than just wanting to tell a story. Storytelling is having a love and full appreciation for the art of telling a story and how the story is created from its inception. Storytelling is an appreciation for the way someone else tells a story and for how it sounds and how it appears in short form, on the big screen, or in a novel. How was this story told and how might you tell it? What makes this story a failure? Storytelling is more than just words, words, words.

› **BEVERLY BARTON**   Most people will agree that there are different types of writers, but many of us fall under the category of natural-born storytellers. We were born with stories in our minds and characters running rampant in our brains from the time we were children. Even before I knew how to read and write, I made up stories. By the time I was nine, I had written my first book. Writing comes as naturally to me as breathing. Storytellers don't necessarily paint poetic pictures with their words the way true poets do; instead they relay stories that draw the reader into the action and make the reader care about what happens to the characters.

› **JOANN ROSS**   I believe we're all born storytellers. If you watch infants babble to themselves and toddlers having conversations with their stuffed animals, you can see the wealth of creativity humans are born with.

Then, about the time children start going to school, they learn to color inside the lines—that the sky is blue, the grass is green, and no, you can't have a separate desk for your imaginary best friend. Little by little, that storytelling ability drifts away. Most of the writers I know have somehow managed to stay in touch with that inner child who's never heard of such a thing as an internal editor.

› **WILLIAM LINK**   Story is the strongest element in writing. Structure seems to be the great weakness in our current movie fare. I found at Universal when I worked with relatively new or young writers that were generally good with dialogue, character development, atmospherics, but crippled telling a story.

3. Being a Natural Observer

The greatest thing a human soul ever does in this world is to *see* something, and tell what it *saw* in a plain way.—John Ruskin

Pulitzer Prize–winning poet and Columbia and Harvard professor Mark Van Doren observed, "If you want to do something for a child, get him in the habit of noticing and remembering things. . . . Our very word 'see' has two meanings—to see with the eye and with the mind." The important thing to glean from Van Doren's words here is that with training, the power of keen observation and remembering what we see with our eyes and mind can be taught and mastered.

I had an interesting conversation with a dog trainer of Irish border collies. She told me that some of these amazing animals are born with something called "keen eye." Their eyes are so intense and focused on what they are doing that when they herd cattle, the cattle respond more to the collies' eyes than any other body function. Not all border collies have keen eyes, however. They must be born with this gift.

The lesson here is that we do not have to be natural *born* observers to be natural observers. Unlike the Irish border collie, we can develop keen eyes.

As writers, we have to train ourselves to notice what is around us, breathe in what is around us, and understand how it relates to the world. Start becoming aware of the obvious and the trivial. Become conscious of the things that mean so much in our daily lives that, by most, don't ordinarily get the attention deserved.

› **T.M. MURPHY** The small things are the ingredients that transform a good story into a great story. Jerry Seinfeld and Larry David were masters of observing the little things and making them universal so we all say, "I know exactly what they're talking about."

I always keep a notebook with me, and I hit my local coffee shop, Coffee Obsession, every morning to observe the characters and listen to the dialogue around me. Be open to what's around you and write it down. Who knows when you'll use it!

› **MARY BALOGH** The ability to create realistic characters obviously depends very largely upon one's ability to *observe* other people. Being an introvert is probably an advantage here. But it is not enough merely to look and listen and get to know people from external signs, however detailed and accurate one's observation is. It is more being able to put oneself right inside the body, mind, and soul of another person, to be able to imagine what it is like to be that person. True understanding and empathy can come only from that type of observation.

Characters in a book can seem as real as living persons to the reader if the writer has the gift of portraying them from deep within, from the level of their very being, with all the myriad factors that have made them the unique individuals they are.

› **STEPHANIE KAY BENDEL** Three people look at a river. One is a marine biologist, one an artist, and one a civil engineer who specializes in designing bridges and dams. They're looking at the same thing, but they're certainly not *seeing* the same thing.

You can use this principle to good advantage in your writing because readers enjoy seeing the world through different eyes. Give your characters interesting careers, hobbies, or experiences that enable them to see the world from particular points of view. A helpful reference is *Careers for Your Characters: A Writer's Guide to 101 Professions from Architect to Zookeeper*, which includes professional jargon, daily schedules, what people of certain professions wear to work, and more.

4. Embracing Solitude

The writer must teach himself that the basest of all things is to be afraid; and, teaching himself that, forget it forever, leaving no room in his workshop for anything but the old verities and truths of the heart, the old universal truths lacking which any story is ephemeral and doomed—love and honor and pity and pride and compassion and sacrifice.—William Faulkner

The word "solitude" might in itself connote only loneliness to some, but it also means "alone." And there is a big difference between being lonely and being alone. I am alone when I write, but I am rarely lonely. I am with my characters and my ideas in the fictitious world I have created and where I am in total control. I am also with my deadlines and my joyful anticipation in knowing that the ideas that I have preserved on paper today will help bring tomorrow's ideas to the fore.

Nevertheless, even with all these companions, writing can on occasion be a lonely business. I cherish this emotion, however, because I can now sympathize with a character who is lonely or fears loneliness. I can create a stark setting that evokes loneliness because I simply become the conduit to expel such emotion. Finally, when I scratch out these emotions onto the page, they are real and heartfelt, and the reader will know that they are not contrived emotions.

› **CINDA WILLIAMS CHIMA** A fiction writer is never entirely alone. Her characters are constantly whispering in her ear. Writing is not a social endeavor. It requires solitude—a meeting between you and your characters on their turf. Some of us can find solitude in a crowded café or the local mall. And none at home.

> **BRUCE BALFOUR** Writing a novel is a lot like poking out your own eyes with a flaming stick. A "real" writer will develop the discipline to do it anyway, instead of just talking about the story to anyone within hearing range. Unfortunately, this requires spending time alone with yourself. Locking yourself in a room without distractions is usually the best course. Woody Allen said that he can't even write in a room with a window.

For the novelist, the key is often to write in the same place, during the same hours, with the same lucky pen or lucky computer, even if only for a few minutes each day until that discipline becomes ingrained in your soul. When you feel guilty about missing your daily writing ritual, you'll know you've succeeded. Don't fear the flaming stick; your eyes will grow back the next day.

> **MARY BALOGH** It probably helps to be an introvert when one is a writer, to enjoy one's own company, to prefer solitude and silence to the social scene. There is almost no way writing can be anything but a solitary business.

It need not be a lonely activity, though. When one is writing, one ought to be able to disappear into the world one is creating and find it and the characters peopling it as real as—or more real than—the world in which one has one's daily existence.

5. Having a Driving Reason to Write

Desire is the key to motivation, but it's determination and commitment to an unrelenting pursuit of your goal—a commitment to
excellence—that will enable you to attain the success you seek.—
Mario Andretti

You must have some motivation to write. This motivation can
be borne from money, the passion to tell a story, or simply to see
your name in print. For example, as Sherwood Anderson's first
publishers would learn, his inspiration to write came not from
the desire to earn money, but simply came from his *desire* to
write. In Clifton Fadiman's *The Little, Brown Book of Anecdotes*,
he tells us that when Anderson's first publishers began to send
him weekly checks to relieve him of the financial burdens that
they thought inhibited his writing, Anderson actually lost his
interest in writing altogether. After a few weeks of receiving the
checks, Anderson returned his latest check to the publisher with
the enclosed note, "It's no use, I find it impossible to work with
security staring me in the face."

But what if you're no Sherwood Anderson when it comes to
money? Perhaps you're more like Earl Derr Biggers, the creator
of Charlie Chan. When Biggers bought a raccoon coat on an
installment plan and then lost his job, his reputation was at stake.
He didn't want to be known as someone who couldn't meet his
obligations. To raise money, he wrote *Seven Keys to Baldpate*.

Whether you are from the Anderson or Biggers vein is not
important. What motivates you is subjective, and the only thing
that really matters is that you have some authentic desire to
write.

> **R.A. SALVATORE** There's way too much pain in this business
for anyone who doesn't *have* to write. I always tell beginning
writers, "If you can quit, then quit. If you can't quit, you're a

writer." I'm not being facetious. The idea that writing is a way to get something else, be it fame or fortune, is ludicrous. The odds are astounding, and I'd wager that they're even more astounding against someone who doesn't love the power of the word.

> **JOHNNY D. BOGGS**   It's called a mortgage. That may come across as flippant, but it's true. I write for a living. No trust fund. No retirement. No steady paycheck. I approach writing like a job. Shower. Go to work in the morning, knock off, if I'm lucky, at late afternoon.

> **MARY REED MCCALL**   Sometimes motivation is just the joy of finding that perfect phrase to capture the moment or emotion you're hoping to convey. Other times it's a character clamoring in one's subconscious or a story idea that blooms to life unexpectedly. When writing is a carefully cultivated habit, it can take on a life of its own, so that if it is suddenly or even temporarily abandoned, it can leave the writer feeling empty and incomplete. Most people are capable of writing, but those with a driving reason for doing it are most often those that take up the pen or sit down at the keyboard and produce over the long term.

6. Believing You're Talented Enough

Belief ain't for sissies.—Peggy Noonan

Believe that you can write the novel you want to write. If you overwhelm yourself with thoughts that your novel will never get published before you have even written it, you have already defeated yourself. Believe that you can write a novel and believe that you can write a good one. The most important thing is to get it written. Believe in your originality. Believe in your ideas and characters. Thinking positive produces substantial dividends.

> **T.J. PERKINS**   If you don't believe in yourself and your story, no one else will.

> **CARLY PHILLIPS**   Believe: This is the greatest gift you can give yourself. Even in your darkest moments, find that sliver of light and believe. You write therefore you are a writer. Keep at it and be proud.

> **MARY BALOGH**   Writing can be learned to a certain degree. You can educate yourself about all sorts of things, such as grammar, plotting, and pacing. However, I believe that there must be an innate talent if one is to be a good writer. The craving to be a writer from childhood on, the insatiable need to read anything and everything as you grow up, the urge to write lengthy stories even as a child, the ability to live in your imagination as comfortably as you live in the "real" world (or more so), the tendency to weave stories out of the people and incidents surrounding you—all of these are signs of talent.

And if you have the talent, you must believe in it and in yourself more than in all the experts and critics upon whom you may be tempted to lean. Shut yourself up alone in a room and come out when you have a completed book!

> **SUZANNE BROCKMANN**   I *never* said, "*If* I get published . . ." For me, it was always *when*.

7. Being a Voracious Reader

The way to get started is to quit talking and begin doing.
—Walt Disney

"Voracious" means to be very greedy or eager in some desire or pursuit. When it comes to reading, greedily devour anything you can get your hands on, not just novels. Read newspapers, magazines, biographies, the directions to your iPod. You can cultivate ideas and voice from any writing medium.

UCLA screen writing instructor Lew Hunter says that he will read anything that comes down the pipeline. If he's eating breakfast and there's nothing else nearby to read, he'll read the ingredients of a cereal box.

> **BILL PRONZINI**   Read as much as you can in the field of your choice. Study how different authors create conflict and suspense and how they achieve their effects.

> **WILLIAM LINK**   I always read, mostly to fill in the time when I'm not on the script, and funnily enough there are many times when I read something that helps me in the writing. Serendipitous? I really don't know. But you might try it.

> **JOHN MCALEER**   While working toward my doctorate at Harvard, I was taught that you will learn more about writing from one hour of reading than you will in six hours of writing. Having taught English literature at Boston College for more than half a century, I can always tell if a student is a reader by the way he or she writes.

> **CINDA WILLIAMS CHIMA**   I sometimes meet fiction writers who tell me they don't have time to read fiction. That's appalling! Reading great fiction is like taking a writing workshop from a master for free.

> **JOAN JOHNSTON**   What is the one mistake most beginning writers make that's the easiest to correct? New writers don't read enough before and while they're writing. No class can teach you to write a book. Novel writing is about telling a story. We learn

to tell stories—plot, character, conflict—by "listening" to stories. The more you read, the better writer you're liable to be. You always get told, "Write what you know." I'd add to that, "Read what you want to write."

› **S.J. ROZAN**   read read read read read read read read read read read. If it means less TV, less family time, fewer movies, whatever it means. READ READ READ READ READ READ READ READ READ READ READ.

› **KIT EHRMAN**   I read with an eye toward improving my writing. I like to "read up" by reading authors whom I admire, whose work I aspire to emulate. You never stop learning.

› **TOM SAWYER**   I cannot imagine being a writer without *loving* to read. One of the very best pieces of advice I've heard given to would-be writers came from an agent, speaking at the Palm Springs Writers Conference some years back. The agent opened his talk by asking how many people in the room wanted to become successful writers. All seventy-five or so raised their hands. After a dramatic pause, the agent said, "Then, from this moment forward, you *will, every day* of your life, read the *New York Times*." He was dead-on correct. Flat-out—if you are serious about being a writer—*any* kind of writer—the *Times* is about as important as your pen, your thesaurus, or your word processor. Now, obviously, very few of us are going to read every word. But you will *invariably* find items of interest and value.

Okay—but—for writing better *dialogue*? Yes. Sprinkled through the *Times* are contemporary quotes, columns about language and usage, and information about everything else that's *happening*, from music to the arts to science and technology, to publishing and on and on. You will *absorb* what's going on in the larger world.

The *New York Times* is, both in breadth of coverage and the quality of its writing, simply the best in the world. By miles and miles. No other newspaper comes close, and I guarantee that once you become hooked on it, you will become a better writer, not just of dialogue, but of *stories*. I cannot begin to estimate how many of the ideas for the 100 produced television scripts and scores of series and movie pitches I've written were inspired by items I've read in the *Times*—from book reviews to news stories to obituaries. *Everything* in it is better written than *anything* else you will find—anywhere.

Further, because the people who produce the *New York Times* take their work *very* seriously—they regard the *Times* as *The Newspaper of Record*—the publication will inform you on subjects and on levels that will amaze you. Not incidentally, it will likely tell you more about what is going on in *your* part of the world than will your local papers.

And the blessing is that in all but America's most remote spots, you can receive home delivery of the national edition seven days per week, or you can access it online. I urge you to do so. It will change you, your perspective, *and* your writing. Profoundly.

8. Being Passionate about the Craft

To tend, unfailingly, unflinchingly, towards a goal, is the secret of success.—Anna Pavlova

Writing is a craft and an art. If you are a writer, you are an artist as much as is an oil painter, sculptor, or ancient stone mason. Your passion for words and sentence structure should equal a painter's passion for color and brushstroke. Take pride in knowing that what you are giving readers is your best work. Like a true artist, never be satisfied that your work cannot be improved. There will come a time when you have to pass your manuscript on to your agent, editor, or friend, but don't ever fool yourself into believing that it is perfect. Almost invariably, once an author's novel is published flaws will surface, but such flaws make professional novelists more passionate than ever to improve their next work.

When I heard Shamus Award winner Dennis Lehane speak at Boston College, he paraphrased Humphrey Bogart's mantra "All I owe anyone is a great performance." Lehane said this is the bar he sets for everything he writes.

> **JOANN ROSS**   I firmly believe in the "three P" philosophy of writing: passion, patience, and persistence. I also believe that of the three, passion is the most important. It's passion for storytelling that gives us our purpose, drives us to learn, and keeps us working, long after publication, to master our craft.

Passion is what keeps us writing through the difficult times (and all writers have them!). It's the passion shining through in our stories that makes people we'll probably never meet want to read them. It's passion that pushes us to the edge, which is a place where we writers sometimes need to be. As Kurt Vonnegut said, "I want to stay as close to the edge as I can without going over. Out on the edge, you see all kinds of things you can't see from the center."

Conversely, lack of passion will also show in your work. And most important, if you don't have a burning passion for writing, how can you expect anyone else to be moved by what you write?

> **CINDA WILLIAMS CHIMA**   If you want to be a writer, you must be in love with the process of writing, whether you achieve financial success or not. There are much easier ways to make a living. Many would-be novelists don't care much for writing, per

se, but are in love with the idea of publishing. If that applies to you, find something else to do.

9. Being Passionate about Novels

I don't know how many times I have read the Nero Wolfe stories, but plenty. I know exactly what is coming and how it is all going to end, but it doesn't matter. That's *writing.*—P.G. Wodehouse

One of the most passionate people about novels that I've ever heard of is retired Army Infantry Colonel Stanley F. Scholl, who served in both World War II and the Korean War and always carried novels with him wherever he travelled. In fact, the night before D-Day, Colonel Scholl spent the entire evening reading Nero Wolfe.

Cherish novels, especially *your* novel. Take delight in knowing that someday your novel will likely be serving someone in a time of need, such as an elderly person who feels alone or a teacher who wishes to share with her students the whole new world you created with your passion.

› **JULIA LONDON**   If you want to write compelling fiction, you have to love compelling fiction. Reading fiction is the springboard for new story ideas and ways to use language to evoke emotion. Novels are the bread and butter of your craft. You must eat to live your dream.

› **CINDA WILLIAMS CHIMA**   Writers should read good novels twice. The first time, read for pleasure. Enter the dream of fiction and stay there. If the book is stunningly good, read it a second time to find out the *how* of it. Reading for craft takes the juice out of fiction, but it is a fabulous way to learn how to write well.

> **WILLIAM LINK**   When I lecture, I tell the mystery writers if they're interested in clever clues and unique surprises that they should read old masters such as John Dickson Carr, Ellery Queen, and Erle Stanley Gardner. The contemporary people to study are Ross MacDonald, Michael Connelly, and P.D. James. They are experts at credible characters part and parcel of beautiful, intricate structures.

> **KIT EHRMAN**   I study the masters and try to figure out how they do it. And I never stop studying because what's special about writing is that there's *always* something new to learn.

> **JILL BARNETT**   I believe that most creative people are drawn to the arts, and writing is a fine art. Once you discover a love of books, when you read a story that sweeps you inside and carries you along in a marvelous experience of living adventure through a character, I believe something physical happens to you. You can feel the story in your blood and nerves; it stays with you, sometimes for years.

We quote from books. Movies are made from books. Musicals are made from books. Much of our religion and spiritual belief comes from books. Books can help us understand who we are and why we do what we do and think what we think. Books teach us about life and humanity. Sometimes books can remind us we can overcome all that life throws at us. Books entertain us, and I cannot imagine a life without books.

> **JOANN ROSS**   I can't remember not reading. My mother would put picture books in my crib and has told me that before I could talk, I'd babble as I turned the pages, apparently telling stories to go along with the pictures.

I wrote my first novella, a tragic romance about two star-crossed mallard ducks, when I was seven years old. Growing up in a remote ranching town in southern Oregon, where the Cascade mountains blocked television signals, the county book-mobile was my lifeline to the outside world. We may have been miles from the nearest highway, but through those novels I traveled to Oz with Dorothy, into the depths of the Grand Canyon with a donkey named Brighty, and to the Kentucky Derby with Old Bones, the Wonder Horse. I hung out in Sherwood Forest with Robin Hood, viewed the glittering wonder of Ali Baba's treasures, sailed the Seven Seas with Sinbad, and sat at King Author's round table.

As I grew older, I continued to read several novels a month to explore worlds and also ideas. This is why one of my favorite quotes is from Christopher Morley: "When you sell a man a book, you don't sell just twelve ounces of paper and ink and glue, you sell him a whole new life. Love and friendship and humor and ships at sea by night. There's all heaven and earth in a book."

> **ELMORE LEONARD** George V. Higgins's *The Friends of Eddie Coyle* set me free. It loosened up my writing, taught me to get into scenes quicker and concentrate more on realistic sound in writing, what Higgins called "the nuances of ordinary speech."

Chapter 2

COMMITMENT

10. Understanding the Downside of Being a Novelist

Writing is the hardest way of earning a living, with the possible exception of wrestling alligators.—Olin Miller

Writing a novel can be all consuming. Your every thought seems to focus on your next plot twist, doubts that your ideas are any good, or maybe the constant fear of the blank page. Bills have to be paid. Kids have to be fed. And, on top of these, you have concerns about publisher's deadlines and fears that no one will like your work. You may begin to panic over the revisions your agent and editor have asked you to make—by the end of the week. Harsh as it may seem, this is only the beginning.

When you finally get your novel published, you'll worry about what critics will say or if your book will even be reviewed at all. Will your readership feel as if you let them down with this new effort? Will your publisher want to publish your next book? You have put in the long hours, made the sacrifices. You wrote all afternoon instead of watching the big game with your family. You ate dinner by your computer, or worse, you skipped dinner entirely, and in the end, your book doesn't sell like you thought despite all the publicity efforts you put into it.

These are just some of the downsides of being a novelist. The chances are quite good that you will experience all of them and more. But when you have gone through them all, begin writing your next novel.

› **JILL BARNETT**   The biggest downside to being a novelist is writing the novel. Because fine and talented writers make it look easy, most people think it's just a matter of stringing words and thoughts together. But it isn't.

› **JO BEVERLY**   Never believe that the fiction writing life makes sense, or will one day make sense. It's insanity by definition.

› **REBECCA BRANDEWYNE**   Writing is an extremely difficult career. The odds of becoming a bestselling author via traditional publishing are slim. Indeed, the hard reality is that the average writer in the United States cannot earn a living solely from writing. Even the latest technology has not changed that fact, nor is it likely to in the future.

› **R.A. SALVATORE**   Remember when you were in the second grade and you wrote something you thought was the best thing ever written? Then it came back from the teacher covered in red marks, destroying you. That's what being a writer is, every single day. Particularly with the Internet and the loudmouths it inspires, a writer will hear constantly how much he/she sucks. And the bigger you get, the worse it will be. So if you don't believe in yourself, you'll be another of those writers who walks around with his head down, thoroughly depressed. I know a lot of writers, but I know very, very few happy writers.

11. Committing to a Career, Not Just One Novel

If you think you can, you can. And if you think you can't, you're right.—Mary Kay Ash

One of the most inspirational stories ever told is the story of Dumbo the Elephant. Throughout most of his young life, Dumbo was persecuted for having big ears. As a result, he hated his ears because they always brought him down. One day, however, he falls from an airplane to his certain doom, but then something amazing happens. Dumbo begins to flap his ears, and he can fly! The very things that had brought Dumbo down his whole life are now lifting him up.

When I first began to write seriously, I was having Dumbo problems. I was just beginning my career as a lawyer, and it was getting in the way of my writing. I wanted to write a novel, get published, make some money, and sit back in a posh office and write novels. It didn't happen, so I had to practice law. Then something amazing happened, I had something to write about. Practicing law gave me my first book, then my second book, third, and fourth.

Many novelists do not write as a career, but this does not mean that they aren't career novelists. Being committed to your actual career is not a detriment to writing. It just might be the very thing that lifts you off the ground.

> ❯ **KAT MARTIN** Being committed to a career and not just one novel is crucial to becoming a successful writer. A publisher is looking for an author he can build. The odds of your first book hitting the bestseller list are slim. But if you are committed to a writing career, to writing books over a period of years, the odds are far better that you can be built into a successful author.

12. Having Precise Goals, Not Just Wishes

Those who dream by day are cognizant of many things which escape those who dream only by night.—Edgar Allan Poe

Wishing that you could write a novel will not make it happen. Don't be a Hamlet. That is, you must be an actor not a reactor. Wishing that you had more time to write will not make you a novelist. You will not have more time. You have the same amount of time as the single mom or dad who just became a bestselling novelist.

Each day you must set some time aside to write even if it is only enough to write one paragraph, or one page, or to sketch out your next idea for a chapter. By setting reasonable goals, you also develop a rhythm to your writing. You will be surprised that once you set a goal of say, one page a day, and you stick to that goal, it becomes part of your everyday schedule.

› **ED GAFFNEY** Anyone who has written a book knows that it's impossible to write a book. Four to five hundred manuscript pages? With a full-time job, a spouse, kids, dogs, and crazy Uncle Louie who can't let go of last year's Super Bowl? Come on.

But it's very possible to write one manuscript page. So just do that. And then tomorrow, do it again. And do it again the next day. In fact, never let a single day go by without writing at least one page. Keep that up, and in a little more than a year, you'll have yourself a finished manuscript. Nice going.

And if you find the time to write two pages a day, heck. You'll finish in about six months—without losing your job or getting divorced. You're on your own with Uncle Louie though.

› **BILL PRONZINI** Write, write, write. Set aside a block of time that fits your schedule and stick to it faithfully. It needn't be more than thirty minutes a day, nor the amount of new work created more than a few sentences. The discipline and the production of *some* wordage at each and every sitting is what is vital. It's easy to find excuses not to write; successful authors don't give in to such excuses.

> **VICKI STIEFEL**   When I sit down to write, I have no goals, quantity-wise. Some days, I only write a double-spaced page, maybe 250 words. Not much! But it keeps that muscle working and the brain (and story!) going. Other days, I can write three to four thousand words. Okay, not often, but when I do, it feels great. And I wouldn't be able to do that if I didn't write every single day.

> **PETER LOVESEY**   Make your writing a regular duty. Remember that one page a day—say 300 words—each day for a year gives you a 109,500-word novel.

> **CARRIE VAUGHN**   Set goals you have control over. "I will write two pages a day and finish my novel by the end of the year" is a good goal because you have direct control over accomplishing it. "I will sell my thriller for a six-figure advance and hit the *New York Times* bestseller list" is a terrible goal because you have no direct control over either of those things. You're bound to fail and become depressed because of it.

13. Holding True to Your Dreams

Change everything, except your loves.—Voltaire

A few years ago, I heard a music producer speak at Harvard University. The producer told a story about a band manager who many years ago represented a small pop band that he hoped would one day cut a record. The manager had numerous connections in the record industry, but every time he played the band's demo tape to a prospective producer, he received a rejection. In fact, he literally exhausted every record label in his country, receiving rejections from every single one of them.

Desperate, the manager finally tracked down a producer of comedy records, the producer I was now listening to. As a favor to the manager, the producer agreed to give the band an audition. When the producer heard the band, he didn't think they were very good, but he decided to give them a chance for two reasons. First, he could see how much the members of the band truly believed in themselves and their work. Second, he thought they were funny. The band? John, Paul, George, and Ringo—The Beatles.

You must believe in yourself to get published. If you harbor too many self-doubts to write your novel or quit halfway through, then you have produced nothing. Your work and ideas are as good or better as the other guy's. Dream big and hold on to your dreams.

› **JULIA LONDON**   Listen to your voice and your gut and keep the flutterings of delight you discovered when you began to write in your heart.

› **JOANN ROSS**   After years of study and practice, a young violinist finally got an opportunity to have his work judged by a world-famous maestro, who told him, "You'll never have a career in music. You have no fire."

The young man eventually got over his disappointment, went on to have a nice career, married, and had a family he loved very much. Many years later, the maestro, who was now a very old man, returned to town to play a concert engagement. The man went backstage, introduced himself again and said, "Years ago I was hoping that I'd be able to live my dream as a violinist, but when I played for you, you said I had no fire. I've gone on to have a good life, a wonderful family, and a successful career. But I've always wondered. How could you tell, in that brief time, that I'd never play professionally?"

The old man shrugged. "I tell that to all young musicians," he answered. "If you'd truly had the fire, nothing I could have said would have stopped you from fulfilling your dream."

Keep your eye on the prize, keep the passion for writing burning, hold fast to your dream, and don't stop writing. And never, ever, forget that to achieve the incredible, you have to attempt the impossible.

14. Being Professional

There is a difference between conceit and confidence. Conceit is bragging about yourself. Confidence means you believe you can get the job done.—Johnny Unitas

Commit to being the most professional writer that you can be. If you want to write and publish like a professional, your work must look professional, and you must have the confidence of a professional. Learn how to put your work in manuscript form, how to craft a query letter, and how to structure a synopsis. You must also know how to professionally submit your work to an agent and editor. If your submission looks like you are an amateur, chances are you will be treated as one.

> **MICHAEL WIECEK** *Everything* you write should be written well—not just submissions, but office memos, Christmas letters, and e-mails, absolutely everything. Practice good grammar, thoughtful construction, and original metaphor all of the time, and it will become a habit. If you dash off meandering, run-on, badly punctuated paragraphs, it will be that much harder to dial up quality when you need it.

› **KAT MARTIN**   Being a professional writer means writing when you don't feel in the mood. It means setting specific hours for work, and then *working*. There is no time for writer's block, just as a carpenter doesn't have time for carpenter's block.

› **CYNTHIA RIGGS**   Treat your writing as if it's a job. Don't wait for the muse to strike. Work at a regular time, in a regular place, and for a regular amount of time, whether it's a half hour or eight hours.

› **BEVERLY BARTON**   Published or unpublished, if you want to succeed, learn to work at writing the way you would any job. Set yourself up a schedule, something suited to your lifestyle and temperament. Go to your office at the same time every day (even if that office is a corner desk in a bedroom or kitchen), sit down in front of the computer, and write. Just do it!

› **JOANN ROSS**   An important thing to keep in mind is that while editors like brilliant authors, they love prolific ones. This means you're going to need to show up every day prepared to work, the same as you would any other job. Can you imagine calling a plumber or the fire department or showing up at an emergency room with a heart attack and being told the people just didn't feel like working that day?

15. Being Willing to Work Hard

Tyranny, like hell, is not easily conquered; yet we have this consolation with us, that the harder the conflict, the more glorious the triumph.—Thomas Paine

If you think that you are going to write a novel, publish it, and retire to a penthouse where you spend the rest of your leisurely days fishing, lunching, and tapping out bestsellers, you're in for a rude awakening. While writing a novel is worthwhile and rewarding, it is a physical and mental challenge.

I appeared on a writers' panel with Dana Cameron and Susan Oleksiw, two highly successful novelists. The participants were there to learn how they could be novelists. To open the discussion, Oleksiw informed the audience that each panelist worked full-time jobs in addition to being novelists. I could tell that the future novelists were a bit shocked. Most novelists have to steal snatches of time and make great sacrifices to get their work done. The work is hard, but the reward is great.

› CARLY PHILLIPS   There is no substitute for hard work, i.e., sitting down at the computer and writing no matter what you feel like doing instead.

› KAT MARTIN   Making sacrifices is part of the job. For example, if you want to go on vacation instead of to a conference, stay an extra few days, but go where your career dictates.

› KIT EHRMAN   Getting published takes a tremendous amount of hard work and tenacity. All the talent in the world won't be enough if you aren't prepared to put in hours and hours and hours of hard work. Writing is damn hard work, filling that blank page, tweaking, editing, reworking, scrapping an idea and going back to the drawing board, again.

Some nonwriters romanticize the profession, which is neat, but it's not reality. Writing takes over your life. If you're lucky, it takes over your soul.

16. Setting a High Standard of Excellence

If a man can write a better book, preach a better sermon, or make a better mouse-trap than his neighbor, though he builds his house in the woods the world will make a beaten path to his door.—Ralph Waldo Emerson

The great motivator James Keller made this keen observation about entertainment: We do not expect all "cream" in our entertainment, but we do expect that the "milk" will not turn sour.

I think people have this same expectation when they buy novels. They know that a novel may not be perfect, but they have a right to expect that it will be enjoyable, thrilling, or thought provoking. Readers have the right to expect that the author has set a high standard of excellence. Set your own bar high.

> **WILLIAM LINK**   A friend, one of the great comedy writers, has what he calls the Eleventh Commandment for writers: Write better. Pass it on.

> **JULIA LONDON**   Writing is an art, but it's also a business. If you want to succeed in this business, you have to strive for the highest standards. The cream floats to the top; the pulp settles at the bottom. A lot of writers swim somewhere in between, but if you strive to be the very best, and every bit of work you submit is the best you can make it, you will eventually be floating in the cream. If you're really lucky, maybe you'll be among the cherries.

> **JOANN ROSS**   I once had a very insightful editor who said that one of the reasons writers are never satisfied with their work is because they're always striving to do better. I've never met a writer who won't admit, at least privately, that no book ever quite lives up to that perfect, ethereal vision we all have in our minds when we first conceive our stories.

Part II
CREATIVITY

In Greek mythology, the muses are the nine daughters of Mnemosyne and Zeus. It is their job to watch over and inspire poets, musicians, and artists. Desperate for inspiration? Don't be afraid that you won't find your muse. If you put a serious effort into your creative work, then you will have plenty of "divine" help.

Keep in mind though, that the muses will not come to you on their own. You must keep writing to let them know that you seek their divine counsel. Perhaps you should hold a special devotion to Calliope because she is the chief of the muses. And thankfully, there are modern-day "muses" we can seek counsel from too.

Chapter 3

THE CREATIVE PROCESS

17. Finding Inspiration

A thought is often original, though you have uttered it a hundred times.—Oliver Wendell Holmes

I enjoy this quote by Louis L'Amour and hope it inspires you to find inspiration for your ideas: "Ideas are everywhere. There are ideas enough in any daily newspaper to keep a man writing for years. Ideas are all about us, in the people we meet, the way we live, the way we travel, and how we think about things."

> **JILL BARNETT** If you try to write by summoning your muse, you will probably not write or ever finish a book. Muses can be elusive things, imaginary beings who carry all our ideas and best work locked in treasure boxes, which they delight in hiding from us. And no amount of magic will ever summon a muse. Writing muses are the biggest of fairy tales and pure fiction.

Technique is what gets you writing. Understanding your craft is the true magic and your safety net. I know this to be true because for almost eighteen years I chased my muse, and she forever outran me—until I was forced to just tell my story without her.

> **JENNIFER BLAKE**   Think of your muse as a super-sensitive friend. She'll be pleased to join you if you're playing soft music, nibbling chocolate, burning scented candles, sitting or lying in a comfortable position, looking at a nice view or neat office, or writing in a daily journal—any situation in which you're relaxed and enjoying what you're doing. She'll stay away if you're stressed out, over-tired, angry, or working only for money. Be kind to her, show her entertaining projects, and she'll sit beside you and whisper in your ear. Abuse her, bore her, and she'll be gone.

> **JOANN ROSS**   You can't sit around and wait for your muse to show up because muses are, by nature, unpredictable, quixotic, cranky, and sulky. They're also occasionally brilliant, which is why we put up with them.

> **TOM SAWYER**   By definition, losers are those who wait for inspiration. Or, put another way, they sure as hell aren't writers.

18. Coming Up with Ideas

I don't wait for moods. You accomplish nothing if you do that. Your mind must know it has got to get down to work.—Pearl S. Buck

Your mind is as Plato contended: the world of ideas. Your mind is truly limitless and so are the ideas that surround you. As you train your writer's mind, you will develop a keen eye for mining ideas, but you will probably become overwhelmed with ideas for a novel, a new setting, and more characters than you can probably use. Sometimes ideas come from a major story in the newspaper, and other times they come from the most trifling of incidents. The key is to train your mind to find ideas and to realize that they can come from anywhere. As you hone your idea-detector, you will quickly learn that finding ideas is not difficult. Ultimately it is how you *use* these ideas that makes all the difference.

> **LINDA SANDIFER**   Most writers will never live long enough to use up all their ideas. Picking the right one to pursue is the hard part. You must choose based on the marketability of the idea. Publishers are always looking for something new and unique, but only if it is a story with broad appeal.

> **JOANN ROSS**   I've always found ideas everywhere, but my favorite place is Nordstrom, because of their liberal return policies for those ideas that don't work out.

> **SABRINA JEFFRIES**   Ideas are like fireflies; go hunting for them and they elude you. Sit and enjoy the night, and they appear from out of nowhere. You have to let the ideas come to you. Expand your world, read outside your comfort zone, take walks. The fireflies *will* come. Just give them the chance.

> **JULIA LONDON**   If you were born to write, ideas will come to you. You will get them from books, movies, songs, and conversations. You will get them from people on the street, gossip, and officemates. Ideas may not come with regularity; they may come in a landslide. But they will come. Don't sweat it; sit back and absorb. If you are the panicky type, have someone with whom you can brainstorm. Bouncing ideas off another person will always get the creative juices flowing.

> **MILES HOOD SWARTHOUT**   When starting out, don't worry so much about your place in the literary hall of fame. Try to pinpoint the most commercial darned topic you can think of, research the hell out of it, polish endlessly, and take feedback from as many pros as you can talk into reading your early work,

and maybe you'll break into print and have a successful first publishing experience, too. It worked for me!

Whether my second novel and sequel will find favor with the gods of show business, that's too much of a crapshoot to worry about. Just stick to the basics and concentrate on what you can control, telling an exciting, commercial story well.

And as they say in Lost Wages—Good Luck!

19. Exploring the World

Continue to expose yourself to new ideas. Trust your instincts and think for yourself. Make art, or at least value it.
—Samuel L. Jackson

I think Jane Austen's words on this subject are extremely useful. "'Only a novel' . . . in short, only some work in which the greatest powers of the mind are displayed, in which the most thorough knowledge of human nature, the happiest delineation of its varieties, the liveliest effusions of wit and humour are conveyed to the world in the best chosen language." I never understood the writer who shuts himself out from the world and then thinks that he can accurately write about the real world around him.

As writers, it is our duty to be part of the world, and also to convey that world to our readers. Take historical novelists who pore over book after book and document after document to enter the historical world they wish to bring back to life for their readers. These authors are not isolating themselves; they are taking a journey through time entering a world once lived and giving it back to their readers as accurately as possible. Really think of Jane Austen's words as she describes a novel: ". . . the greatest powers of the mind are displayed, in which the most thorough knowledge of human nature, the happiest delineation of its varieties, the liveliest effusions of wit and humour are conveyed to the world." As a writer, you want to live and write by these words.

> **STEPHANIE KAY BENDEL**   Make use of your own experiences. Travels, full- or part-time jobs, and bits of trivia all can be rich sources for fresh perspectives for your characters.

> **JAMES F. MURPHY JR.**   Travel has been a great teacher for me—Asia, Europe, Canada, and the United States.

> **JOHNNY D. BOGGS**   If I can, I try to travel to the area I'm writing about to spend some time soaking up local flavor, so to speak, and studying the land.

> **ROBIN MOORE**   I think one of the reasons that my book *The French Connection* became a *New York Times* bestseller and subsequently an Academy Award winner, is that I spent so much time getting to know Eddie Eagan and Sonny Grasso—the real-life New York City detectives who cracked the French connection heroine syndicate. Because I worked so much with my writing subjects, both Eddie and Sonny were real on the page and therefore real on the big screen.

20. Being Open to Experiences

A writer is working from the instant the alarm clock goes off to the moment when he goes to bed. For that matter, the [creative] process does not stop when I'm asleep. The old subconscious mind takes over then and sifts things around and sets the stage for the next day's work.—Lawrence Block

One day, I went to make a deposit at my local bank. Little did I realize that I would experience something new. I learned what it was like to carry $1,000 in quarters. Doesn't sound like much? Well, it was worth its weight in gold to me.

I saw the assistant manager with two huge clear plastic sacks of quarters on his desk while he was filling out forms. I jokingly asked him if he had change for a dollar, and he retorted that he didn't have any change on him. I asked him where all the quarters came from. He said that because the bank is next to a Laundromat, they end up with sacks and sacks of quarters. I asked him what happens to all the quarters, and he told me that they go to the Federal Reserve. He added that the old man from the Federal Reserve always became grouchy at the bank because he hated toting the heavy bags out to the truck. I asked the assistant manager if I could pick up one of the bags to experience what it felt like to tote one around. I figured this was the opportunity to experience something I never done before, and it wasn't going to cost me a dime. By lifting the bag, I could experience what the curmudgeon guard from the Federal Reserve experiences each time he has to carry one of them.

From this experience, several character ideas were borne: the hard-working Laundromat owner keeping track of each quarter, the cranky Federal Reserve guard who has had it with the bankers and Laundromat man, and maybe the terrible bank robber who tries to escape with the heavy booty. I don't know what I will do with all this new and exciting information, maybe nothing, but it is stored in my writer's bank, ready to withdraw should I ever need it for a short story or scene.

Try to experience as much as possible. That doesn't mean that you have to travel the globe to obtain material to write about. Experience the world as much as you can, but not at the expense of the area around you. Take in the small details of your community, the day-to-day grind of people you do business with every day, but have never really taken the time to notice. Take notice of life! Then go write about it.

> PETER LOVESEY Give your writing the authentic feel by using your own experience. Of course you don't have to commit a murder to write about one, but you can give it a strong sense of place by choosing a setting you know. Dorothy L. Sayers worked in advertising and wrote *Murder Must Advertise*. Agatha Christie trained as a pharmacist and used her knowledge of poisons in her books. P.D. James worked in the police department at the Home Office. Colin Dexter, the creator of Inspector Morse, is a champion crossword solver and a lover of real ale and Wagner.

> ROBIN MOORE Be a proactive writer—an adventurer. As Ernest Hemingway said, "Live it up so you can write it down." I have to agree with Hemingway on this. My best work came after I wrote *The Green Berets*, where I actually trained with the special forces and served with them in Vietnam. I was nearly forty at the time; it is never too late to live it up and write it down.

> BRUCE BALFOUR Whether you're writing about the mean streets of Austin, Texas, or the pedestrian slipways of Beta Centauri IV, you should spend some time explaining the common environmental details of your fictional world to create a definite sense of place for your reader. If your urban protagonist wakes up in a gutter in San Francisco with his face on gritty concrete and his body stretched out on a warm asphalt road near a fish market, it's a different experience than waking up in a gutter in Buenos Aires, where the streets are paved with cool granite cobblestones and a dog is barking in his ear. The reader needs to experience the world through all five senses of the character. Getting these details right will enhance the reader's immersion in the story and make your fictional details more believable. Getting these details wrong will elicit letters from outraged readers who live in those places and know you've never been there. This is particularly disturbing when they live on Beta Centauri IV.

› **KIT EHRMAN** Writing is an interesting form of self-enter-tainment, but I need to come up for air and join the real world or I'll run out of raw data, be that character inspiration or story ideas. Because I write about the horse world but no longer run a barn, it's important for me to occasionally immerse myself in that world, to slip back into its intricate, beautiful rhythms. So, I visit that world whenever I can to recharge my batteries. On a deeper, more psychological level, if I'm not living real life and experiencing real emotions, I probably don't have much to say that's truly genuine.

› **JOANN ROSS** Writers all need to do extensive research on locations and other details intended for our books, but I also believe it's important to get away from the computer from time to time because you never know when everyday interaction with "real" people will make its way into your stories.

For example, the writers for *Cheers* supposedly hung out in bars and wrote down conversations they'd overhear. This is partly why, I suspect, the dialogue in that show always sounded so spot-on. I don't know any writers who can go out to dinner without eavesdropping on conversations at surrounding tables. Those conversations often spark new ideas.

I once worked in an ER on the Fourth of July. Thirty years later, I tapped into memories of the turmoil and organized chaos of that day—when it seemed ambulances were never going to stop arriving at the hospital—for my novel *No Regrets*.

Another time, I saw a woman hanging clothes on a line on a quiet residential street near San Quentin prison. The domestic scene, in such a startling beautiful location where you could see the death row gas towers, had me wondering if the tidy homes—many with Private Property, No Parking signs stuck in their lawns—belonged to people who worked at the prison. If so, weren't they, in some way, perhaps nearly as much prisoners to the place as the inmates? That mental image stuck with me for nearly twenty years and triggered the San Quentin prison scenes that eventually ended up in my romantic thriller *Blaze*.

Live your life with your eyes wide open and soak up the amazing world around you. You never know when something seemingly insignificant at the time will provide the all-important final piece that completes your novel.

21. Studying the Market

Not knowing when the dawn will come I open every door.
—Emily Dickinson

A young man wanted to be an actor, so he showed up at a local theater to give it a shot. The powers that be (TPTB) pointed out to him that he couldn't read and that with his accent he couldn't be an actor, so they sent him packing. Not one to be swayed this easily, the young actor went out and took a job as a dishwasher. With his first week's salary, he bought a $13 radio. For six months, the actor listened to the radio whenever he could and repeated what he heard to improve his accent. He became a sedulous reader, reading even during his short breaks as a dishwasher, and taking tutoring lessons. At the end of the six months, the actor went back to the theater, and TPTB agreed to let him stay on a trial basis. But at the end of his trial basis, TPTB did not invite him to return. Still not swayed, the actor asked if he could stay on to do janitorial duties in return for theater lessons. Reluctantly, TPTB gave him a chance to sweep up. The young man got his "nose under the tent" as they say and eventually landed some roles at the theater. He exhibited enough talent to eventually get a break in Hollywood, where he would go on to win an Academy Award and the Screen Actors Guild's highest honor, the Life Achievement Award. The actor is considered to be one of the finest ever to take the stage and fill the big screen. The young man who swept the floors to get his chance to sweep the viewing hearts of moviegoers is Sidney Poitier, now himself a *New York Times* bestseller.

The lesson here is: Do your homework, do what you have to do to put yourself into a position where TBTB can't say no.

> **PETER LOVESEY** Study the market. Go to a bookshop or the library and get a sense of what is being published now.

> **MICHAEL BRACKEN** While it's important to keep abreast of market trends, no writer should slavishly follow trends. It's better to write the books you want to write.

22. Knowing What Makes a Great Story

In my belief, you cannot deal with the most serious things in the world unless you also understand the most amusing.
—Winston Churchill

My friends Tom and Ruth had me over for dinner one night, and their four-year-old daughter, Maureen, began telling me about a birthday party she went to that day. Ruth told me that there had been a storyteller at the party. When I asked if he was any good, Ruth gave a lukewarm review. Then I asked Maureen how she liked the storyteller, and she instantly flashed a big smile. She said that she really liked him and that he was funny.

Based on these two reviews, I would have to say that the storyteller knew what made a story great because, in large part, he knew exactly what his audience wanted. His job was to make the children happy and to get them to enjoy the stories. There are of course formulas to stories and plot, but what can make a story great is how you go about telling it in your own unique way and knowing what your readership wants to enjoy and how they want to enjoy it. If you capture your readers' or audiences' imagination and they think that your story is great, who can say it isn't?

> **MARY BALOGH**   I am not sure there are any rules about the art of telling a story, though the "how-to" books doubtless list many. If a story grabs the reader from the opening page and holds that reader until the last page, then it has been told well. How does the writer do this? I am not sure there is a definitive answer. As a rule-of-thumb, I usually judge my own work by asking if it excites me, if it draws me back day after day until I have finished telling the story. I always assume that if I am slightly bored, then my readers almost certainly will be.

> **JAMES M. CAIN**   To me, a story has to have some *objectivity* beyond subjectivity. . . . I like a narrative to be concrete, not all inside some person. Of course a story, a good concrete narrative, has to be about particular people. They have to have problems that we can understand and believe. It seems to me that a good narrative moves objectively.

23. Writing about What You Love

Imagination is more important than knowledge.—Albert Einstein

Many an aspiring writer has stared at a blank screen, wondering what on earth she should write about. Spending time worrying that you must complete your novel now or you will miss the latest trend is a surefire way to sabotage your belief. Instead, write the novel *you* wish to write—the novel you would love to write—and create the characters you feel comfortable with. Trends come and go and if you try to latch onto a trend it will likely be passé by the time you have completed your manuscript.

› **T.J. PERKINS**   I know you've heard it a million times, but it's so true. Write about whatever it is you like: mystery, fiction, true-to-life, fantasy, etc.

› **LAWRENCE BLOCK**   Write only what you want to write, the way you want to write it.

› **SABRINA JEFFRIES**   Too many beginning writers think shorter automatically equates with easier. The truth is, it's just shorter. Short fiction takes a whole different set of writing skills and can actually be harder to write if your bent is toward novels. Write what you really want to write. If you love long, complicated tales, don't waste time trying to master a short form.

› **KIT EHRMAN**   My number one rule is, "Write what you love." If I can do that, I've moved a ways toward mastering what readers enjoy because, after all, I'm a reader, too. I love suspenseful mysteries with heroes I can fall in love with or, at the very least, find sympathetic. And if that story is set in an interesting world with an insider's look into a fascinating job, so much the better. I'm happiest when I feel the need to check that the doors are locked and the curtains are drawn because the book I'm reading late into the night has me spooked.

24. Writing about What You Know

Writing what you know is good for the soul. Writing what you don't know isgood for the mind. In either case, if done well, it's good for the reader.—Heather Hall-Martin

Shortly after I graduated college, the mother of one of my friends asked me what I was going to do. I said I didn't know.

She responded by saying, "Well, just remember, it's not *what* you know, it's *who* you know." This trifling exchange altered the course of my life, but not in the way you might imagine.

I thought then, and I still think now, that her philosophy on how to get ahead was cynical. I was determined to get a job on my own, and I did. I landed a job with a major health care company in Boston working with doctors, nurses, and mental health professionals. It was my first white-collar job, and I was making less than $19,000 a year. Still, I felt like a millionaire. And how did I get this job? Well, it wasn't because I knew somebody. I got it because I knew how to mop floors.

One day I walked into the health insurance building armed with a few résumés and asked to speak with someone from human resources. A woman came out, and I introduced myself and told her I would like to be a claims adjuster. She asked what office experience I had. I told her that I had none, but that I had been a custodian in a nursing home in high school and college. Her face lit up, and she told me that she didn't have a claims adjuster position for me, but she needed people who were familiar with what it was like to work in hospital facilities. I interviewed with a nurse and because I had picked up an incredible amount of medical terminology while working in the nursing home, it was easy for me to converse with medical professionals. I was an anomaly: I may not have known how to run a board meeting out of the corner office, but I could speak their language, so they hired me.

Not long after, I was promoted to the contracts department where I developed an interest in law, so I started to go to law school at night. Ultimately my interest in criminal law led me to want to write a novel. Now, I'm not so naïve to think that there wasn't a little bit of luck thrown in here, but like the poet said, "Luck is the residue of hard work."

The point is, while *who* you know might be important, often it's *what* you know that will open doors for you, in your work and also in your writing.

> **S.J. ROZAN** Write what you know. But not what you know on the outside. What you know on the inside. If you're a dental assistant, your character doesn't have to be a dental assistant. If it's always burned you up when people are sweetly patronizing about your work, write about a seething character. If you live in Wyoming on an isolated ranch where loneliness sometimes feels like it's crushing you, write about a guy in downtown Chicago who can't connect to anyone.

> **BRUCE BALFOUR** "Write what you know," writers are often told. You can't take this old saw too literally. I've written about Mars and ancient Egypt, but I've never been there. Presumably, Tolkien never went to Middle Earth or met any hobbits before he wrote *The Lord of the Rings*. William Gibson introduced the term "cyberspace" in *Neuromancer*, describing virtual worlds and artificially intelligent computers, without even owning a computer. Stephen King has never shot a U.S. President or experienced a massive plague.

Direct experience is great, but secondary sources of information, if you read enough of them and check your facts, will often suffice. Personalities and character interactions can certainly be based on people you know, but even there you don't want to stay too close to the original model. The details of your accountant's daily life probably aren't all that interesting to the average reader unless he's a serial killer planning to murder all of his clients.

> **JOANN ROSS** I'm a firm believer that contrary to conventional wisdom, writers should not write about what they know, because there's no excitement of discovery in doing that. Instead,

write about what you *want* to know, because your enthusiasm will shine through and be contagious to your readers.

25. Joining a Writer's Group

Any time you see a turtle up on top of a fence post, you know he had some help.—Alex Haley

You can build a worthy ship alone, but you don't have to. Likewise, you can write a good novel alone, but you don't have to. Because writing is such a solitary activity, it can be helpful for several reasons to join a writer's group. A good group can motivate you to get going, help you develop ideas, work with you to avoid any troubling roadblocks in your novel, and encourage you to keep writing when you're lacking motivation.

Finding a good group is key, so search hard. If a group is interested in your story and characters and if they care enough to want to hear your work and resolve any difficult areas, it's likely a good fit for you.

› **CYNTHIA RIGGS**   Writing is a lonely profession. Join a writers' group. If there isn't one near you, or there's one you don't like, start your own. Ask your public library to post a notice and meet at a neutral place, such as the library. Limit the group to no more than seven. Make sure criticism is positive (not personal) and give participants equal time.

› **CINDA WILLIAMS CHIMA**   The most important thing you can do to improve your writing is to find a good critique group. Honest, loving critique is a gift to be treasured. Join a writing organization, take a fiction-writing class to link up with other writers, put a sign up at the library—whatever it takes.

› **LINDA SANDIFER**   Some writers like to brainstorm or belong to critique groups. When first learning your craft, this might be helpful, but I think too much of it can cripple a writer. A writer can find herself trying to please everyone in the group until she loses her direction and her own voice. Learn to write your *own* story and trust your own judgment.

› **MARY BALOGH**   Here's a word about critiquing groups or reading partners or other ways in which a writer may involve others in the creative process: All writers are very different from one another, and therefore I would not set down anything as a definite rule, but my advice is to keep strictly alone until the work is complete to your own satisfaction. This is a work of art, and it comes from your talent, experience, value system, and very being. It has your unique and distinctive voice. You ought to be very wary of allowing anything in that might contaminate or upset the balance of those precious facts. Get advice—even follow it if you choose!—after the work is finished, but not before.

26. Attending Writing Classes and Workshops

O gentle Reader! You would find A tale in everything.
—William Wordsworth

Writing classes and workshops are held all over the country, in schools large and small. Sure they require investments in time and money, but most writers believe that classes and workshops can be helpful.

If you choose to attend one, keep this advice in mind. The old adage that there is no such thing as a bad question is true. Nevertheless, some questions are better than others, and yours ought to be. Have one or two good questions prepared—questions that will elicit valuable, thought-provoking advice.

› HANK PHILLIPPI RYAN I began writing as a solitary endeavor. No one—except my tolerant and patient husband—knew I was writing a mystery novel. After thirty years as a television reporter, I figured I knew how to write stories and decided writing a book would be just like writing an extra-long story.

About a month into it, I realized I was wrong and how much I didn't know. I devoured books on writing, and I took a wonderful (and pivotal) mystery course from the master, Hallie Ephron.

› JULIA LONDON Attend writing workshops. Learn all you can about the craft. Network, listen, and ask questions. But don't adopt every rule or suggestion tossed out. Take what fits; discard the rest.

› SABRINA JEFFRIES Never enter a workshop expecting to find answers to your burning writing questions. Workshops are for offering you tools and teaching you how writers work. Some of the tools will be useless for what you do (while wildly helpful for other writers). Other tools will change your world. Be skeptical of writers who try to tell you that you can't be successful without mastering their particular tools.

› LIZ CARLYLE Resist the urge to go to workshops and ask authors anything at all. Listening to someone else explain how *they* write can take the edge off *your* voice, and your voice is all you have to sell. This advice is a bit tongue-in-cheek, of course. Workshops can be useful tools, but the question to ask is: Can you go and listen with a discerning mind, sort the wheat from the chaff, and take home only that which will strengthen and complement the skills you already have? Or will you let your insecurities undermine your confidence in what you already know in your writer's heart?

> **JOAN JOHNSTON**   I encourage anyone who wants to write to join a writer's group and attend conferences where the craft of writing is taught. There are lots of ways to improve your story through craft—for example, going for the choke when you're writing an emotional scene and writing with a hook at the beginnings and endings of chapters to write an unputdownable novel.

> **JOANN ROSS**   One problem I have with workshops is that too many people will latch onto something and think it's a rule. To quote W. Somerset Maugham: "There are three rules for writing a novel. Unfortunately, no one knows what they are."

Chapter 4

THE WRITING ENVIRONMENT

27. Finding Time to Write

When one door closes another door opens; but we so often look so long and so regretfully upon the closed door, that we do not see the ones which open for us.—Alexander Graham Bell

Some authors are morning writers, others afternoon writers, and still others night writers. A few lucky writers can write anytime. Finding the time can be a challenge for aspiring writers. Most everyone runs out of minutes in the day before they run out of things that need to be done. You may long to write in the mornings, but your kids have to get off to school and banging out a page is just not going to happen between breakfast and bus stop. Or perhaps the only time you have to write will be after a hard day's work, talking into a tape recorder during forty-five minutes of fender to fender. Or maybe you sit down in front of your computer after the kids get to bed fourteen hours after you crawl out of bed. Make a commitment to carving out time in each day for *you* to write.

› **MICHAEL WIECEK**   As the father of two young children, my writing time depends entirely on their schedules. I do most of my writing after the kids go to bed.

› **LORI HANDELAND** My favorite time to write is any time that I have. I began writing when I had a three-year-old and an infant. I wrote early in the morning, late at night, and any time I could steal during naps. As my children got older, I exchanged playdates with other mothers or left them my children one hour longer at daycare and snatched my time then. I remember those hours as blissful, crammed full of my characters, my plots, and my love of the process.

› **MICHAEL BRACKEN** When my children were small, I did most of my writing late at night, after they had gone to bed. Now that I'm an empty nester, I do most of my writing mid-day. I like having sunlight streaming into my office, and I like looking out my window whenever my fingers pause on the keyboard. I find that I have fewest interruptions in the afternoon, when there's nothing on television that will distract me from writing.

› **ROBERT GOLDSBOROUGH** Unlike many of the writers I've talked to, I don't have a set writing schedule. When I still held down a full-time day job, I was by necessity more disciplined in my writing: I'd work early in the mornings or late at night. Now that I'm retired, I tend to be more scatter-shot in my writing times.

Also unlike some writers, I can make use of relatively short blocks of time for my writing—even an hour or less on occasion. This probably comes from my experience as a newspaper man. I didn't have the luxury of sitting in front of the typewriter or word processor agonizing for long stretches. I had deadlines and had to start right in. That mindset still holds for me, and I'm almost always able to start writing the moment I sit down.

28. Finding a Place to Write

I find that what I write when I force myself is generally just as good as what I write when I'm feeling inspired.—Tom Wolfe

A quiet office with a big mahogany desk and comfy swivel is the dream of many authors, but the reality is, you may have to be content with being a nomadic writer. For many writers, it is best to learn to write wherever and whenever you can. My first few manuscripts were written longhand in lab books during breaks when I sanded floors and worked as a substitute teacher. Sections of the book you're holding, in fact, were written on legal pads while I was waiting for an ultrasound. That extra hour the doctor kept me waiting was not wasted; the foresight to bring my pen and legal pad paid off. Even though I *can* write on the run, I still *dream* about my perfect writing space, and in some ways I have one. When I transcribe my longhand work, I sit at my computer in my office where I can—most of the time— enjoy a quiet, comfortable, and inspiring place to write.

> **JOHNNY D. BOGGS**   I typically write out of my home office, but I've also written drafts in my car, on Amtrak, in an airport, on an airplane, and in a hotel room. It's my job, and I'm blessed to have a job I love.

> **HANK PHILLIPPI RYAN**   During my thirty years as a television reporter, I got used to writing news stories on wet notebooks in the middle of hurricanes, with mittened hands as the snow swirled, and jouncing in the backseat of a news van on the way to make a deadline. Of course, it's easier at my desk, and writing novels is much more civilized at your own computer or under a tree with a yellow pad or wherever your favorite spot is.

Writing a novel is all about getting it done, but it's very easy to put it off. You say, I'm at Mom's, on vacation, too hot, too hungry, or at an unfamiliar computer, and then the time goes by, and your book is unfinished. A hundred little delays have added up to blank pages.

When I'm on the trail of my own plot and the lives of my characters, nothing can keep me from writing, wherever and whenever. The thrill of having a good idea and getting it down means some chapters get written on the backs of envelopes while riding the subway or in the blank back pages of someone else's paperback. Transcribe your ideas later. Get them down now.

> **JOANN ROSS** It's been said that if you want to write a novel, you should go in a dark room, lie down, and wait for the feeling to pass. However, if you're one of those people who can only write in an absolutely quiet room with no distractions, get over it! I used to think those prison writers who occasionally get published had it easy. All they have to do is sit in their cells and type away while other people wash their clothes and feed them. Then I realized prisons were even noisier than my house, so there went my plans to get arrested.

29. Assembling Your Writing Tools

Beware of all enterprises that require new clothes.
—Henry David Thoreau

As in any trade, the tools you use are important. It is equally important that you know how to use them and feel comfortable with them.

While most writers write at computers today, some still prefer the rhythm and clacking of typewriters. In fact, not too long ago I watched a *60 Minutes* segment about Danielle Steel—one of today's most prolific and successful authors—and it showed her hammering away at a typewriter! Other authors still write their first drafts longhand. Try new methods of writing to see what works best for you.

For me, my computer is an extremely important tool, but what I consider to be equally important is my backup system. Computers crash; be ready for it. When you punch in the word "end," you want it to be the end of your story, not the beginning of starting over because you erased your work.

You'll also need a good dictionary. I keep two dictionaries—one old and one modern—in my office as well as an old and new legal dictionary. My old law dictionary dates back to 1912 and contains numerous Latin phrases that my new *Black's Law Dictionary* does not.

I would also feel helpless without my *Familiar Quotations* by John Bartlett. My version dates back to 1955, and it contains many scholarly quotes that have been removed from the new printings. I need to buy the updated version, but I'm holding on to my old one for sure. I'm not going to find quotes from John F. Kennedy or Bill Cosby in my 1955 printing, but then again, I will find some nice ones from Ben Franklin that didn't make the cut for the recent printing.

Finally, my most important tools—other than my mind—are my tea kettle and trusty mug. They have pulled me through many a blank page and plot snare.

> **PETER LOVESEY** Get the right tools for the job. By that I don't mean a word processor. You need a good, modern dictionary and some reference material. For example, if you want to write crime, get some up-to-date accounts of policing and forensic science.

> **ROBERT GOLDSBOROUGH** In my early years publishing fiction—the mid-to-late 1980s—I wrote on a typewriter, somewhat reluctantly moving to a PC with the onset of the '90s, but

I'd never go back. The ease of editing and rewriting on the computer easily override any nostalgia I might have for the "good old days" of the sturdy old manual Smith-Corona or even the IBM Selectric.

> **MICHAEL WIECEK** I wrote my first novel on a typewriter, but everything since then has been fully screen-based, including notes, plot cards, timelines, and all the other detritus that never appears in a finished manuscript.

But for plotting, character notes, and so forth, a pencil turns out to be a remarkably versatile tool. Make sure you get one with an eraser. The biggest advantages of a pencil are that it is always on, and you can write in any place and in any position. Pens always seem to run dry when I use them lying down in bed, and a laptop's electrical requirements are burdensome.

> **MICHAEL BRACKEN** I'm old enough that I started my writing career using a manual typewriter and had to use carbon paper to make duplicate copies of manuscripts as I typed them. I was ecstatic when I purchased my first IBM Selectric typewriter, and I have used personal computers ever since IBM released its first PC and WordStar was the word processing program of choice.

I'm a Macintosh user today. I've always felt comfortable writing at a keyboard, and I think that has helped me make the transition from manual typewriter to electric typewriter to personal computer.

At the same time, publishers' needs have changed. When I began writing, I submitted manuscripts on paper, later marked copyedited text by hand with a blue pencil, and then proofread typeset galleys before the work was paginated. Today I am more likely to submit manuscripts as files attached to e-mail, editors may edit the files and return them for my approval, and page proofs may come to me as PDF files. I may never see the manuscript on paper until it comes off the printing press ready to ship to readers.

Being comfortable with the technology that allows us to go from the creative process through the production process electronically is especially important to writers today. As an editor, I receive many electronic manuscripts prepared by writers who clearly do not understand how to use their word processing programs. Their files are filled with unnecessary keystrokes that I or another editor have to remove. The failure of writers to provide clean electronic manuscripts is just as bothersome to editors today as the failure to provide clean typewritten manuscripts was thirty years ago.

Chapter 5

THE WRITING PROCESS

30. Developing Your Imagination

The mightiest lever known to the moral world, Imagination.
—William Wordsworth

Did you ever hear someone say that they have no imagination? To me, that's like saying you have no heart. The imagination is there, you just need to go out and find it. Imagination is borne from our observations and experiences, combined and massaged into our stories, characters, and scenes.

Remember that quaint country store you visited in New England? Imagine how it smelled, revisit the architecture in your mind, and recall the other visitors there and what their reactions were to the store. Imagine you're walking around and suddenly you discover a dead body, suddenly it's 1875, suddenly a creature from the planet Trekia pops in to pick up a bushel of caramel apples for his long trip to the planet Kirktune . . . Have faith in your creations, and your imagination will run wild if you let it.

> **KAT MARTIN**   Let your imagination run free whenever possible. I particularly like to do that at night, when I have trouble sleeping, or in the morning when I first wake up.

> **JAMES F. MURPHY JR.**   I suppose I was born with an imagination. I read. I've always been a dreamer. Stories, all stories stimulate me.

> **ROBIN MOORE**   Use your imagination and create scenes that never occurred in real life. I confess that some of the greatest scenes in *The French Connection* movie were not in my book. I had signed a contract to write the book strictly as the case unfolded. But after seeing the magnificent drama on the screen, I decided that whenever possible in my future books I would avoid being limited to bare facts and *factualize* the fiction I wanted to write.

31. Doing Your Research

Whatever is worth doing at all, is worth doing well.
—Earl of Chesterfield

I was fortunate to hear the enormously successful novelist Chuck Hogan (*The Standoff*) talk about his novel *Prince of Thieves*, which was set in Charlestown, Massachusetts. A member of the audience asked him how he was able to describe the Charlestown underworld with such authenticity.

Hogan explained that for nine years, he collected information about Charlestown, visited Charlestown, and interviewed the people of Charlestown. Hogan said that he enjoyed his research immensely. *Thieves* has been a major success, proving that Hogan's long—yet enjoyable—efforts paid off.

Here are two lessons to take from Hogan. First, research is vitally important. Second, don't view research as back-breaking toil. It can be fun and informative, and it can enrich your dramatic sense. When you have done your research right, readers will sense the authenticity of your work.

> **MARY HIGGINS CLARK** Even while I am working on a book, I continue to research. For example, my book *The Cradle Will Fall* is about an obstetrician who experiments on, and sometimes murders, his pregnant patients. I read everything I could get my hands on about artificial insemination, in vitro pregnancies, and fetal transplant experiments. I interviewed and picked the brains of a doctor friend who is a researcher in a prenatal hospital laboratory. I proposed "what if" questions to obstetrician buddies. Then when the book was completed, I gave a copy to an obstetrician friend. We talked on the phone for four hours checking all of the medical references in the book.

> **STEPHANIE KAY BENDEL** Don't forget research. Some years ago, I was asked to write a mystery set in an exotic locale. I had been to Puerto Rico recently, so I chose a hotel there as a setting for "The Woman in the Shadows." But I wanted one of my main characters to be a blind sculptor. I imagined that he'd been an artist who lost his sight and took up clay sculpting. I had to do a bit of reading about blindness, how it varies between people who have never had sight and those who have lost it. I was surprised at how acute the other senses became, so that a blind person often perceives many things that a sighted person overlooks. Learning these things was a real pleasure, and I trust that my readers enjoyed the unusual perspective as well.

> **JOHNNY D. BOGGS** Perhaps one of the biggest changes in Westerns over the past few decades is an added emphasis on historical accuracy. Readers are savvy. They'll call you on a mistake. I start my research with history books and biographies, then check bibliographies and footnotes for primary sources. I'm a big fan of *www.abebooks.com* and the interlibrary in the area where I'm setting my story. I voraciously read period newspapers. You can't always trust the accuracy of the reporting, but

you get a great flavor for language and locale, and the advertisements can be loaded with little details I like to toss into the story for added authenticity.

> **PATRICIA BRIGGS** The little details matter a lot—so no guessing. When you are writing fiction (particularly speculative fiction—science fiction, fantasy, and horror), it is important to make your world utterly believable. The minute you get a detail wrong, it pulls your reader out of your story.

For instance, if my characters are riding horses through the woods in the autumn and notice the apple blossoms, immediately the astute reader (who knows apple trees only blossom in the spring) is reminded that she is reading a story written by someone—when that is exactly what I want her to forget. If there are too many of these "world building" mistakes, your reader will no longer trust you or believe in your story. So get it right.

For example, I don't know plants, but I know people who do. My husband is terrific at running down obscure experts. He once contacted the curator of weapons at the Metropolitan Museum of Art to find out if bluing a sword would damage its temper. I've talked to police officers, learned to shoot guns, and read books on obscure topics to make sure I get it right. I may write fantasy, but when I have an extreme tide that pulls me out miles from shore, I know exactly how it works before I put it in.

> **ROBERT GOLDSBOROUGH** Because my current series, the Snap Malek Chicago mysteries, is heavily historical and mixes real people and events with fictional ones, I usually start by doing several weeks of research. Once I have determined the period in which I'm going to set the story, I go to the library and pore over the microfilm of Chicago daily newspapers from the specific time, say early 1938 or fall 1942, to get a general sense of the era and a specific sense of the events of that period.

For anyone writing historical fiction set in the past 150 years or so, I highly recommend newspaper files—either microfilm or bound volumes—to get a feel for the era.

> **LINDA SANDIFER**   The proper amount of research will enrich your story, but too much will bog it down. You can also research a topic to death and never get around to actually writing.

32. Becoming Possessed by the Story

So many of our dreams at first seem impossible, then they seem improbable, and then, when we summon the will, they become inevitable.—Christopher Reeve

Once you have a story idea and begin to write, you can become possessed by your idea. You will become focused and develop an overwhelming desire to complete your manuscript. Everything you see, hear, and do will have you asking yourself how these things could be worked into your story. This is a good place to be. Now that you are possessed, more than ever you begin to anticipate what it will be like to actually complete your first manuscript. You'll want to see how your book will end. You'll have a burning desire to know how it will feel when you tap in that last bit of punctuation. You'll wonder, what will it be like to see the clean pages of your first *full* book-length manuscript float out of your printer? You will want to know what it is like to say, "I did it. I wrote a book!"

> **CINDA WILLIAMS CHIMA**   Writing fiction for me is very much like reading. I have to go on to see what will happen!

> **REX STOUT**   I know pretty much what my main characters are like, but beyond that I just have to wait to see what comes out of

my typewriter. I make up one-third of the things people say and do in the stories I write, but I have nothing to do with the rest.

> **LINDA SANDIFER** My now-adult children confessed that when I was working deadlines, they would wait until I was deeply engrossed in my writing to ask for something because I would consent to anything and never remember it later.

> **KIT EHRMAN** It's easy for me to drop off the grid when I'm writing. I immerse myself in a fictional world where I'm god. I'm in control, creating a story that's as dangerous and exciting or romantic as I like, and it's oh so easy to get wrapped up in that world. And I'm having fun with the characters I've created. Let's face it: We can come to know a fictional character more deeply than most of the real people in our lives.

33. Nurturing Your Creativity

You can't wait for inspiration. You have to go after it with a club.
—Jack London

One way to nurture your creativity is to do some good, old-fashioned work. I have always found that one form of work nurtures another. While writing or working on a legal matter, I am at least subconsciously laying out my tomato garden or thinking about the old-fashioned replica wheelbarrow I want to make.

Conversely, performing manual tasks is a great and relaxing way to work out a plot kink. While sawing wood, it might suddenly come to me how the suspect gives himself away. The professional writer is always writing.

Another way to nurture your creativity is to try new things. Try writing short stories or poetry, painting, singing, dancing, creating flower arrangements, or redecorating. Just like different exercises build different parts of your body, different artistic activities will build your entire creative self.

> **MICHAEL BRACKEN**   True inspiration is rare and valuable, but waiting for it to strike is a fool's game. The best ideas come to writers who are actively writing and not daydreaming.

> **BEVERLY BARTON**   I'm one of those writers whose head is filled with so many ideas that if I lived to be 200, I'd never have time to write all the stories, so if I lose an idea or two, it's no great loss. If an idea hits you, write it down ASAP. I've written a paragraph, a page, even an entire scene and filed it away. Some I've used, some I haven't. But you never know when one of those flashes of genius will hit and the idea will inspire a bestselling novel.

> **MARY HIGGINS CLARK**   Where to get the *idea*? Easy. Pick up your local newspaper. The odds are that on the first page or two it contains news of at least one homicide, an aggravated assault, a bank robbery, a mugging, a jailbreak. There also may be a recap on a criminal trial that merits national attention, an update on a series of unsolved murders, and an item about a child who has been missing. In other words, you'll find material for a dozen short stories or novels.

34. Recording Your Ideas as Soon as They Appear

If a man has a talent and cannot use it, he has failed. If he has a talent and uses only half of it, he has partly failed. If he has a talent and learns somehow to use the whole of it, he has gloriously succeeded, and won a satisfaction and a triumph few men ever know.—Tom Wolfe

While you can train your mind to be creative, don't let your creative ideas slip into oblivion. Carry around a small memo pad and pen or small tape recorder to capture your ideas as they come.

Ideas for your story can come at any time. Maybe you have a chapter idea or a scene idea, but it won't take place until much further down the book. Don't fret. You don't necessarily have to wait until you get to that chapter to get this new, brilliant idea down. Get it penned now and preserve it. You may not end up using it, but the bottom line is, you have done some good writing and practice never lets you down. Moreover, maybe you can't use the idea now or you think you won't be able to use it, but as the manuscript begins to take shape, you may find a way to use the idea that you had never intended and, as a direct result, the book now has an exciting new twist that you could never have thought of. Well guess what, you did, because you preserved your idea when you had it and were courageous enough to take a chance with it on paper.

> **LIZ CARLYLE**   You never know when the next notion to go floating through your brain will be the seed for next year's bestseller, so never leave home without scratch paper and a pencil. Keep a digital recorder in your coat pocket and a steno pad on your nightstand. Yellow Post-it Notes work well in damp bathrooms. If you're away from home and caught without, call yourself and leave yourself a voicemail.

When you have pushed yourself deep into the plotting process, those mental snippets can come with startling ease— *annoying* ease when it's three in the morning. Ideas. Names. Plot twists. Cover ideas. Nebulous what-ifs. They will spring upon you when least expected, but that's the kind of wool that can often be spun into pure gold, so don't let it slip away.

› **BEVERLY BARTON**   It's true that ideas flit through our brains at odd hours of the day and night. I've jumped out of bed at night to find a pad and pen so I could jot down a brilliant idea. Sometimes the next morning when I've reread these pearls of wisdom, they've turned out to be hogwash. But once in a while, those ideas turn into books.

› **JAMES F. MURPHY JR.**   I used to forget to write the ideas down. Now I put them to paper. I may not use them right away, but they are there for the future. Don't throw anything away. Keep all ideas.

› **HANK PHILLIPPI RYAN**   When the first line of *Prime Time* popped into my head—fully formed—I was at a restaurant, and the seared tuna was just arriving. I grabbed a paper napkin and a pen and scrawled it before I forgot. Two years later, when the book came out, that line was exactly the same.

I have notebooks and pads and pencils everywhere: on my nightstand, in the car, in my purse, and yes, tucked under my chair at the dinner table. I write down snippets of phrases, words, people's names, lines of dialogue, street signs. Sometimes whole paragraphs will come to me, and I scramble to get them down.

› **JOHN MCALEER**   I could not have written *Rex Stout* without my handy tape recorder. The biography took seven years to write, and I visited Rex a few times a year. With Rex's permission, I recorded countless yards of tape. I used these "notes" for the biography, and I was able to publish a companion to the biography, *Royal Decree*, which contains some of my most memorable conversations with Rex. Hearing his voice over and over again gave me another sense to write with and hence, a better understanding of my subject. Also, I am never without pen and scrap paper when I can help it.

> **GREGORY MCDONALD**   I don't write down ideas, or bits and pieces. If you forget something you thought brilliant yesterday, it is, by definition, not memorable.

35. Collaborating

Union gives strength.—Aesop

I read an interesting article in *www.mystery.net* about two cousins who in 1929 wrote a mystery novel to enter into a magazine contest and won. The cousins would go on to develop a writing collaboration that lasted forty-one years, ending only by the death of one of the writers. They wrote nearly forty detective novels and seven books of short stories. They also created a magazine that some six decades later is still in publication. Their stories would be featured in more than 400 radio programs, nine feature films, four TV series, and two TV movies. This writing venture consisted of Frederic C. Dannay and Manfred B. Lee, a.k.a. "Ellery Queen."

Author collaboration is very difficult, and even if it does work, not every writing team can expect to be as successful and productive as Dannay and Lee. While two heads are better than one, this is not always true in writing. In fact, just the opposite can happen. Artistic differences can waste an incredible amount of time and destroy good ideas. Such differences can lead to nothing getting done at all and the feeling that one partner is doing more work than the other, leading to resentment and bankruptcy of ideas. Nevertheless, if two people can collaborate like soul mates, they can be as successful as "Ellery Queen."

> **MARY REED MCCALL**   A prerequisite for collaborative work is a sense of mutual respect. It's pretty much a given that authors who write collaboratively will disagree at various points along the

way to producing a finished work. Yet with mutual respect, each writer's perspective can be heard, weighed, and either accepted or not from that wonderfully safe place of knowing that the point or issue has been considered with much thought and care.

> **JOHN MCALEER**   In the fall semester of 1965, I entered my office at Boston College and found on my desk a letter addressed to me in a boyish scrawl. The letter writer, William "Billy" Dickson, was serving time in Walpole State Penitentiary for bank robbery. Dickson had seen a copy of a review I had written for the *Boston Globe*, and he had a few questions for me. Thus began our 1,200-letter correspondence. I encouraged Dickson to write about his Korean War experiences, and we put them in the manuscript form of a novel. The novel, *Unit Pride*, was published after Dickson's parole and became a bestseller, hailed as one of the best war novels of all time, ranking it with *All Quiet on the Western Front* and *The Naked and the Dead*.

At the time I was corresponding with Dickson and writing the novel, I was working full time and raising six children under the age of eight with my wife, Ruth. I was criticized by many for collaborating with a prisoner incarcerated for bank robbery, but as a veteran of the Second World War, I knew firsthand how tough it could be for GIs to assimilate back into society, particularly GIs like Dickson who experienced prolonged, frontline combat. I felt Dickson deserved a second chance, and I'd say he made the best of it. I was honored to collaborate with him.

> **WILLIAM LINK**   I am frequently asked by young writers if they should collaborate. Maybe I'm the wrong guy to ask. I met Dick Levinson (fellow *Columbo* creator) the first day of junior high school, and we were a writing team and best friends for forty-three years until his untimely death. (Another tip for writers: Don't smoke!)

Collaboration is great if you are aesthetically and tempera-mentally compatible. Oscar Hammerstein II defined collabora-tion as exactly the same as marriage, but without the sex. In Hollywood, most teams write comedy. There seem to be fewer and fewer dramatic teams these days. Perhaps this is economic as I always warn my inquirers that you will split the money. There is also the problem of spouses. If you get together early and are prosperous when both members are single, there can be a prob-lem when one marries before the other. A spouse can complain that his or her spouse is doing all the work while the partner goofs off. There might be just personality problems. Dick and I were lucky in that regard, very lucky, but I have seen it create real problems with others.

Creatively, two good heads can be better than one. Usually if one partner is at a loss solving a problem, his partner can come through. When Dick and I hit a brick wall, we would retire for the day rather than argue. Always the next morning one of us would have come up with the solution. I will admit to this day that I was blessed having Dick as a partner.

> **ROBIN MOORE** I have published nearly 100 books. Some of them I have written on my own, and others I have cowrit-ten. In fact, some of my most successful works were written with coauthors. I have cowritten novels on treasure hunting, the Mafia, diamond smuggling, gambling, the drug trade, and more. I cowrote one of my latest books, *The Singleton: Target Cuba*, about a solo special forces operator, with retired Major General Jeff Lambert.

I wrote one of my most exciting projects when I lived in New York. I teamed up with controversial madame Xaviera Hollander to write *The Happy Hooker*, which became a successful movie and the bestselling original paperback in publishing history—with nineteen million copies sold. For me, collaboration has been an opportunity to discover and delve into a new facet of life that I had known nothing or very little about.

Of course, there can be drawbacks on a collaboration project. I am, even at eighty-one years young, demanding of myself and my coauthors. I want the facts, and when I set them down on paper, I want them to be right. I owe this to my readers. I still like to rise at 5 A.M., get right behind the computer, and begin my work. Additionally, I am fortunate to have the ability to work on many different projects at once, and when I devote time to a different project, I like my coauthors to understand this. But in the end, collaboration has served me well, and I hope that I have served my readers well and have helped produce books of social importance.

If a project excites me and a coauthor is up for the challenge, I have a difficult time saying no. And I'm glad I do because I have had many adventures as a result.

36. Outlining Your Story

The test of first-rate intelligence is the ability to hold two opposed ideas in the mind at the same time, and still retain the ability to function.—F. Scott Fitzgerald

Novelists and storytellers vary on how they outline stories. Some authors don't outline at all, others outline sparingly, and still others outline meticulously. There are advantages and disadvantages to all of these forms of outlining. Through trial and error, you will discover what type of outliner you are.

By not outlining, your subconscious takes over, and you create something wonderful and unique every time you put a word down on the page. The problem with this form of writing is that like most things you don't plan, you can run into problems that you can't fix, and you may have to go back to the drawing board.

By partially outlining, you give yourself a balanced mix of direction and subconscious creativity. The disadvantage is the same as not outlining at all because you could still run into a problem you can't fix. But at least by partially outlining, you have decreased the odds of potential impediments. By meticulously outlining, you know where the story is going and how it ends. This method can save an incredible amount of time, but was an opportunity lost? If you had just loosely outlined, could the story have taken a creative turn for the better? You'll never know.

> **JAMES M. CAIN**   I make notes for a novel. My notes are an outline, but I write twenty outlines before I get done with it. Then I boil the outlines down to two to three pages of handwritten script. Then I'm done with it.

> **JOHNNY D. BOGGS**   Usually, for a novel, I write from an outline. But the outline is quite loose, sometimes just a couple of words. Often during the writing process, I'll go back and tweak my outline, revising it when I think of something else or realize that the outline won't work. Where I don't use an outline is in dialogue, unless I'm capturing a quote from history. Because dialogue, most often, is spoken off the cuff, I want it to flow naturally. I'll tweak it during revisions to make it fit character, but I don't want conversations to sound staged.

> **CINDA WILLIAMS CHIMA**   I don't do an outline. I usually have a beginning, can visualize a few glittery scenes in the middle, and sometimes know the ending. I develop characters I can believe in, get them in trouble, and follow them to see what happens. I try to be flexible enough to follow them wherever they go.

> **KAT MARTIN**   Whether you outline or not is your preference. If you don't, write a synopsis. Get your story idea down

on paper and expand it as you go along. The more complex your plot, the more details you need.

> **ROBERT GOLDSBOROUGH** I don't usually outline a book before I start, but I do have a general sense of where I'm going with the story. I'll often write short paragraphs describing each of the characters: their vocations, ages, appearances, and personalities. I also create a calendar for the period in which the story is to take place, with boxes for each date of the month. This way, I can avoid such things as having someone in two places at once, which almost happened in one of my Nero Wolfe books!

> **RHYS BOWEN** To outline or not to outline? There is no rule. You have to find out what works better for you. For beginners, it is comforting to see that framework tacked above the desk. I start off knowing very little. I know what sort of environment my crime will take place. I sometimes know who will be killed, and why. But I find the story works better if I let it develop naturally, and not always in the way I had foreseen. It's good to be open to startling new directions and not have to try and work the story back to fit my outline. I do use Post-it Notes on a board beside my desk. For example, I'll note that "We have to know this much by this stage of the book," or "Make sure she has an encounter with x." Then I remove the notes as they come into the story.

37. Choosing Your Point of View

Measure twice, cut once.—Scottish saying

Two young fish were swimming along one morning when an adult fish swam by and said, "Good morning, boys, how's the water?" and then swam away. Later, one of the young fish said to his friend, "What's water?" Like in life, in writing perspective is everything. Deciding what point of view to use to tell your story is a critical decision to make. It's best made early on, to avoid a whole lot of rewriting should you later change your mind!

> **ELMORE LEONARD**   From James M. Cain, I gained an appreciation of the antagonist's point of view: The bad guys are more fun to write about than good guys, their attitude and the way they talk more entertaining. Because I've always spent at least equal time writing from the antagonist's point of view, a friend of mine in publishing would write to ask, "How's the book coming? Has your good guy done anything yet?"

> **KRIS NERI**   I look at my story elements from three angles. First, back story—I separate out the elements that lead up to the crime, just to be sure I don't give too much history, which can slow down the narrative flow, and so I use it to hook the reader. Second, the villain's story—I work out the villain's behind-the-scenes actions—how he carries out the crime, how he establishes his alibi, how he casts doubt on someone else, etc.—by working through it before I write the book. I'm sure there won't be any holes. Third, the story I'll write for the reader—Only after I separate out the back story and work through the crime as it's carried out from the villain's perspective, do I tackle the book's story line, which is from the protagonist's perspective.

38. Plotting

I don't believe in pessimism. If something doesn't come up the way you want, forge ahead. If you think it's going to rain, it will.
—Clint Eastwood

Plotting a novel is tough work. It may be easy to come up with an idea for a plot, but to execute it and structure it in a suspenseful, thought-provoking way often requires what *Columbo* creator William Link calls "Fancy dancing."

From the get-go, ask yourself if your plot idea is suitable for a whole novel, or is it better suited for a subplot, short story, scene, or narrative hook? Perhaps the plot line lies elsewhere. Additionally, ask yourself if your plot idea will work with your characters, setting, tone, and theme.

› **CARLY PHILLIPS** Accept your process. Everyone's process is different. Whether you fly by the seat of your pants or you plot the book to death, accept it before you tear your hair out with each book.

› **PETER LOVESEY** This is a personal tip and may be controversial, but it saves me time and rewriting. Plot before you write. Make sure you have a satisfying story in outline form before you start chapter one. Using this method, I don't put the book through a series of drafts. Each day's output will appear on the printed page. I know plenty of writers who like the challenge of not knowing where they are heading, but this way works for me.

› **ROBERT GOLDSBOROUGH** Most of my fiction writing has been in the murder mystery novel genre, specifically whodunits, in which there usually are four to six suspects. One of the most difficult aspects of writing whodunits for me is to give all of these suspects roughly equal motives for having committed the murder. The idea is to keep the reader guessing as long as possible.

I try to adhere to the doctrine of fair play in the plot. That is, I put in clues so that the reader could conceivably identify the murderer. Having said that, I bury the clues by making them hard to spot. Many of these clues are embedded in seemingly innocuous details.

> **MARY HIGGINS CLARK** The plot, like the foundation of a house, is the structure on which all else is built. No matter how glib the writing, how enchanting the characters, if the plot doesn't work, or if it works only because of flagrant coincidence or seven-page explanations at the climax, the book is a failure.

Now for your own plot. Pick up your local paper and find some interesting case, one that for whatever reason sticks in your mind. Begin a file on it. Cut out every newspaper item that refers to it. *Know* that case. If a defendant is indicted attend some of the trial sessions if possible. And then—and here's the key—use that case as a nucleus for your story. You're a fiction writer, so invent, go further, ask yourself "What if?"

> **CYNTHIA RIGGS** Play fair with your readers. It's not fair to have characters discussing something the reader knows nothing about. And it's not fair to have a totally unexpected ending to your story. Let your reader follow you all the way. Even if you're writing a mystery, plant enough clues so readers can, if they're paying close attention, figure out whodunit.

> **WILLIAM LINK** Never—repeat—never—think that a problem can't be solved. I call this the art of "fancy dancing." Sometimes your solution might be a bit shaky, but it's not worth throwing away a good piece of work because you were nose-to-nose to a brick wall. As any bricklayer will tell you, bricks can be removed. Raymond Chandler threw away whole novels because he couldn't go forward. That man needed help.

> **STEPHANIE KAY BENDEL** Whenever I run into a nagging problem of plotting or motivation that won't go away, I find that sleeping on it helps, particularly when I follow a certain path. First, I try to define the problem in a sentence, such as, "Why doesn't Amanda call the police right away?" or "Why

does Ben resent his son so much?" I find that when I'm awake, such questions often inspire answers that are unsatisfying and predictable. Letting my subconscious solve the problem often works for me.

A case in point is a story I was working on called "A Murder in Perspective." I imagined two young couples who were good friends. The wives both became pregnant at the same time, but one couple moved away before the children were born. A few years later, they got together and discovered that their sons looked so much alike that they obviously had to be half-brothers. I figured that was a pretty volatile situation, and a murder could very likely ensue. I considered various possibilities. One husband kills the other, one wife kills the other, husband kills wife, etc. No matter which way I looked at it, the story didn't feel satisfying.

Then I called in my subconscious. That night as I was falling asleep, I asked myself, "Who gets killed, who does the killing, and why?" By morning, I had the answer: One of the little boys is killed. Who does the killing? The other little boy. Why? Because ever since this little doppelganger appeared, life has taken a turn for the worse. Mommy and Daddy are fighting, the home has broken up, and everyone is unhappy. Primitive thought? Yes. But it's how a child thinks. The story sold immediately.

39. Finding Your Pace

Go ahead, make my day.—Clint Eastwood

Readers are demanding and they have a right to be. If you are marketing your novel as a suspense novel, then it ought to have the pace expected of a suspense novel. If it doesn't, you will hear from readers and your first book may just be your last. Tough, but true. Publishers need to sell books in order to stay in business. How you pace your novel will dictate what type of reader-ship will be attracted to your particular work and will therefore help the publisher market your book to interested readers.

> **R.A. SALVATORE** The most important thing is to find your own pacing. I'd like to say that I know how to do it, but that would be a gross generalization. I know how to do it for those people who want to read a story with the pacing and style that I present. Many people would prefer another style or another pace. Certainly the people who love Robert Jordan's long *Wheel of Time* are getting a different experience from the frenzied pace of a Drizzt book. Different readers want different things. Heck, even the same readers want different things at different times!

> **MARY HIGGINS CLARK** Suspense by its very nature sug-gests an express train or a roller coaster. Once having gotten on board, you cannot get off until the ride ends. I am committed to the belief that this is essential to good suspense writing.

> **JOHNNY D. BOGGS** I don't like excess. I prefer spare writ-ing, but I look for a good flow among the words and paragraphs. I don't like writing that calls attention to itself. I'd rather have a reader remember the story.

40. Getting the Basics Down

The reward of a thing well done, is to have done it.
—Ralph Waldo Emerson

Readers choose certain books and authors for many different reasons. We may like a particular author's characters and dia-logue. Sometimes a book can take us to a place or time that we would not be able to visit otherwise. And sometimes, we just like a good plot twist. As an author, you should try to perfect all of the foregoing. Imagine—you have written a novel with a great setting, the characters are round and alive, the dialogue is pitch perfect, and you came up with a killer plot twist. Get these basics down and the readers will follow.

> **CINDA WILLIAMS CHIMA** Get the basics down first—character, setting, and plot. In fantasy, the world doesn't function according to the familiar laws of nature. But fantasy worlds have their own rules that must be consistently followed. Let the reader know what the rules are early. For example, if Jasmine's going to escape the evil wizards in the last chapter by turning invisible, you better show us that talent several chapters ahead.

> **SABRINA JEFFRIES** You can never know too much about writing. If you *think* you know everything, you're not leaving yourself open to learn. Study how other writers work, especially the ones who move you to tears or laughter or amazement. Try to find out how they did it. Then experiment with those techniques in your own writing. The best writers are always learning, exploring, and trying to improve.

> **BILL PRONZINI** Use adverbs and descriptive adjectives sparingly. Too many of both are telltale indicators of amateurism.

> **REX STOUT** It is always an artistic fault in any fiction to mention other characters in fiction. It should never be done.

> **PETER LOVESEY** Don't be afraid of breaking the rules of English you learned at school. Perfectly correct English can be a bore. So put in the occasional sentence without a verb. Don't worry if a sentence ends with a preposition. And start some sentences with *And*.

> **JAMES M. CAIN** Sometimes if I need a "hell" or a "god-damn" I put it in, but it's like garlic: a little bit goes a long way. And once I use one of them, I'm done with it. And the four-letter words. I think I did use a four-letter word in *The Institute*, where I more or less had to. And in *Mildred Pierce* I used a four-letter word. He said something like she was a "beautiful piece of tail." But mostly, I lay off it.

> **JAMES F. MURPHY JR.** My best editorial hint is read your piece aloud to yourself. Your trained ear will do the editorial work.

> **JOHN MCALEER** Humor can break down doors. As Rex Stout's authorized biographer, I once asked him what, if anything, crime fiction lacked. "Humor" was his categorical response. A little humor goes a long way. People—and remember editors are people too—enjoy a good quip or a humorous anecdote. Put an editor into good spirits, and they may read on.

> **JOAN JOHNSTON** What's the toughest thing for a beginning writer to learn? The only thing that should be left on the page is information necessary to tell the story. Too much extraneous information, such as a desire to show off all that research you did, slows the story down. Less is more. No character should be left in the book who isn't imperative to the plot. The tighter you can write the book, the more exciting it will be for the reader.

41. Creating Characters

When writing a novel, a writer should create living people; people not characters. A character is a caricature.—Ernest Hemingway

Once upon a time, there was a woman who wrote a book about the Civil War and Reconstruction. She had very little faith in her manuscript and kept it squirreled away in her little apartment affectionately know as "the dump." A friend who was upset with the author for not sending out the manuscript, told her that she didn't take her life seriously enough anyway to write a good novel. Put off by this "challenge," the author sent the manuscript off to an editor interested in her story and although he liked it, something about it bothered him. The main character, a female, was off somehow. She didn't fit. The editor suggested to the author that if she changed the character's name, he would publish the book. The author agreed to change the name from Pansy O'Hara to Scarlett O'Hara, and Margaret Mitchell's novel, *Gone With the Wind,* would go on to win the 1937 Pulitzer Prize and sell more books worldwide than any other book except the Bible.

People must relate to and believe in your characters. Scarlett O'Hara could, and did, survive war, lost love and family, and Reconstruction. Would anyone believe that *Pansy* O'Hara could survive Scarlett's challenges? By simply giving this central character her rightful name, a great American character was born. Scarlett became the real person she was meant to be. She became round, not flat—a "living person." The best plot in the world will not save your story if your readers don't care whether or not Rhett comes back to Pansy.

› SUZANNE BROCKMANN Good writing is all about the characters. It's important to make your readers want more than just to accompany your characters on their journeys. Make your readers want to stand, shoulder to shoulder, and fight your characters' battles alongside of them. Then your readers will remember your books and your name. And they'll come back for more.

› JOHN MCALEER Make your works and characters enjoyable, and readers will want to visit your creations again and again.

> **BILL PRONZINI**   Well-developed characters and strong sense of place are vital to any piece of successful fiction.

> **PETER LOVESEY**   F. Scott Fitzgerald once said, "Action is character." Make sure things are happening, and the way the characters react or speak will make them live.

> **PETER LOVESEY**   When beginning to picture a character, I cast around for someone I know. As the story develops, so will the characters. By the end, they are quite unlike the real people I started with.

> **REX STOUT**   A character who is thought-out is not born, he or she is contrived. A born character is round; a thought-out character is flat. Readers seldom give a damn what characters illustrate, or whether they illustrate anything. The reason readers are more interested in my characters than in my plots is that the characters seem real to them and engage their emotions and concerns just as "real" people do. Most characters in stories don't do that. I haven't any idea why and how I have created characters who do.

> **JOHNNY D. BOGGS**   Most editors, critics, book lovers, and other writers say they want a character-driven story, not a plot-driven story (unless they're writing pulp fiction). To me, though, character *is* plot, and plot *is* character. The character, if it's a strong character, drives the plot, pushes the story. What I find in my writing is that although I may be drawn to a story, it's the characters—whether they are historical figures, composites, or people plucked from my imagination—that make the story happen. I don't speak to them, but they are real to me, and I think if they are real to me, they'll turn out real—believable—to my readers.

> **MARY HIGGINS CLARK** Through trial and error, I evolved something of a system of character development that has helped me. The key phrase is *know your people*. Do a biography of them before you begin to write your story. Where were they born? What do they look like? Where did they go to school? What kind of clothes do they wear? Are they sophisticated or easygoing? Are they married? Do they have children?

Think of someone you know, or knew as a child, who reminds you of the character you're trying to create. Remember the way that person talked, the expressions he or she used.

For example, when I was inventing Lally, the bag lady in *A Stranger Is Watching*, I combined two people from my childhood. One was our cleaning woman who used to come up the street invariably singing "lalala"; the other was the proprietor of a hole-in-the-wall candy store near my grammar school. She was one of the homeliest women I've ever known. The boys in my class used to make jokes about calling her up for a date. Together the candy store proprietor and "Lala" as we nicknamed our cleaning woman merged into Lally. Then to get the feeling of authenticity, I haunted Grand Central Station and chatted with bag ladies.

Here's another thought. Hundreds of examples of fine books contradict what I'm about to say, but here it is anyhow. I like to write about *very nice people* who are confronted by the forces of evil and through their own courage and intelligence work their way through the deliverance. Personally I'm not comfortable with the nonhero or nonheroine who is basically so bad-tempered or self-serving that in real life I would avoid him or her like the plague. I don't get emotional satisfaction out of a book in which the villain is so desperately attractive that I find myself rooting for him to beat the system. My villains are—and probably will continue to be—as evil, frightening, and quietly vicious as I can dream them up. I know I'm on the right track if

I'm writing at night alone and the house makes a settling noise, I uneasily look over my shoulder.

Another key element in creating characters is to *orchestrate* them. Within the framework of the plot, try to have a variety of people in whom your readers believe and with whom they can identify. Never, never throw away a minor character. Let your reader understand him, know what makes him tick. And make it a cardinal rule that every minor character must move the story forward.

› **BARBARA D'AMATO**   We've all read books that forced us to look back to try to find out who a character is. The reader shouldn't have to do this. Suppose you are introducing James Smith, the lawyer. You may feel that it will be boring calling him the same thing all the time. But the reader isn't likely to notice and will be much happier than he will by being confused. Some tips:

1. Refer to the same character the same way. Don't call him James in one place, Jim in another, Mr. Smith somewhere else, and Smith Esq. in another spot. Until you're sure the reader knows him, be comfortable calling him something like "our lawyer Jim."
2. Do not be afraid to mention the character's relationship or profession.
3. Give the character characteristic speech and always keep it consistent.
4. Have other characters refer to this character in characteristic ways.
5. Have other characters react to this character in the way you want the reader to react.
6. Connect an event, an argument, or even an object, such as a pipe, to the character.

42. Writing Dialogue

My whole life, I've been a great eavesdropper. The nuances of ordinary speech interest me, but what really fascinates me is the person who is so caught up in what he's saying that he tells more truth than he intends to.—George V. Higgins

I love everything there is about dialogue. Writing it and honing it to its bare, stripped down elements. Reading it, rereading it, discussing it, authenticating it, and ferreting out its subtext. I especially enjoyed stealing it from the blowhard at the corner of First and Third who didn't know that I was tuned into his conversation about the bastard from the East Village Laundry who never returned his fabric softener. And beware, I swipe original dialogue every day, from everywhere, and from everybody that dare come into my path, and you should too. No one should be safe.

Dialogue creates a character's and story's point of view, and it can be used to describe, set tone, develop characterization, and to create humor, sadness, detachment—every emotion possible, just as in real life. What your characters say and how they say it—or don't say it—can tell your readers more about your characters than page after page of description.

> **CYNTHIA RIGGS** Real conversation doesn't translate into believable dialogue. Listen to people talk, but shortcut what they've said when you write by cutting out 85 percent of the words they use.

> **ED GAFFNEY** Brilliant dialogue in movies and television inspires me. I always enjoy watching *The Philadelphia Story* and early seasons of *The West Wing*. Usually, it's just a line, or sometimes even a phrase, that can get my creative heart pumping. A few that come to mind are, "I am beholden to you," and, "There

are rules about things like that" from *The Philadelphia Story*. In *The West Wing*, President Bartlett gives a speech that begins, "The streets of heaven are crowded with angels tonight," and answers one character's inquiry as to the first commandment with the line, "'I am the Lord thy God, thou shalt have no other gods before me.' Ah—those were the days." Hearing characters speak that way just makes me want to get to work.

> **WILLIAM G. TAPPLY**   Don't be afraid to sprinkle "he said" and "she said" liberally through dialogue exchanges. Don't let more than three dialogue exchanges happen without adding an attribution. You do not want your readers to lose track of who's speaking, but attention-getting tags such as "he exclaimed" or "she expostulated" are cumbersome and distracting. Write "he said" directly after the first natural pause in the spoken statement, and it will be virtually invisible to the reader while still signifying who's speaking.

> **PETER LOVESEY**   Listen to the voice in your head. Write it down and then speak it aloud.

Also, don't be afraid to write a stark "he said" after a line of conversation. Cut the adverb that tries to creep in: he said tersely . . . angrily . . . sarcastically. If it's terse, angry, or sarcastic, it will show in the speech.

> **JILL BARNETT**   Read Hemingway. No one told a story better through dialogue than Hemingway. His short stories are the best examples of dialogue you can find: "Hills Like White Elephants" and "A Clean Well-Lighted Place."

Dialogue is tricky because you have to cut the boring dialogue: people greeting each other, everyday talk. Dialogue, like your book, must have conflict and drama, and it must move the story and reveal characters. Recently a new editor told me my dialogue was luminous. She said, "You must read it aloud." (This is an old technique taught to students as a way to write good dialogue.) What this technique really does is help to create an ear for dialogue.

The truth is, I don't read my dialogue aloud and never have. Actually, I'm lucky. I have a strong ear for dialogue and an even stronger self-editor. If the dialogue is wrong, I come to a screeching halt. But like most everyone, when I am first creating a scene or struggling or I haven't discovered my true character yet, I often find I'm writing in someone's head instead of telling through an active dialogue scene. I change the paragraphs fairly quickly.

So, to me the best exercise for writing good dialogue is to sit down and write a scene inside your character's head, telling us something important, then take the scene in a different direction and find a situation where the character must talk about this with someone instead.

Never have characters talk to themselves. Dialogue must be between two or more people, and it is best and most dynamic if it is between two conflicted characters. Create two people with different agendas—or opposite goals—and have them talk to each other about what they want, and your story will move like crazy.

43. Making Conflict Work for You

As you go along your road in life, you will, if you aim high enough, also meet resistance . . . but no matter how tough the opposition may seem, have courage still—and persevere.—Madeleine Albright

Take conflict and spin it into gold.

In 1940, a young law student from Yale was so inspired by a presidential candidate who spoke out against party bosses and patronage systems that he decided to volunteer for his campaign. But when the student showed up to roll up his sleeves, the campaign manager kept him waiting for four hours and in the end snubbed the idealistic volunteer. The student was so offended that after his service in World War II, he decided he would do something about it. The campaign manager was himself a party boss, and the student, now an attorney, decided to run for Congress against the party bosses' candidate, and he won! The attorney would go on to have a very successful career in Congress and become our thirty-eighth president—Gerald R. Ford.

Ford may not have been looking for conflict, but when he found it, he put it to work. Everyone experiences conflict. When you do, put it where it belongs—in your writing.

> **CINDA WILLIAMS CHIMA**   Conflict makes a great story. No conflict—no story. Don't take it easy on your characters. Make them suffer and bleed.

> **TOM SAWYER**   The next time you watch your favorite sitcom or drama, observe that *all* of the scenes are *arguments*. If they aren't, you'll be changing channels in a hurry. Once you begin thinking of your characters in this manner—the ways in which they *disagree* and *don't* get along with each other—you'll quickly find that they *will* talk to you.

The element essential to entertainment is conflict. The challenge is that since childhood most of us have been denying and/or avoiding our own angers. This is something we *must* get past if we want to be writers (or actors or painters or artists in *any* medium). It starts when we're kids. We learn that "boys don't cry," or we mustn't show our anger toward parents, siblings, friends, etc. It's part of the process we all undergo enroute to becoming "civilized." Well, we can't be in touch with our characters' angers/frustrations/passions if we aren't in touch with our own. Stories—both drama and comedy—are about people who are experiencing their emotions. Letting go. That's a *big* part of the vicarious pleasure we take from novels, short stories, movies, plays, and the like. We enjoy watching people who are acting out—because by comparison our own lives and emotions are so dull (read: quietly suppressed). In a way, it's about giving ourselves *permission* to *feel*—a very cathartic process. I urge you to rethink your characters—and your stories-in-progress—in terms of their arguments and/or anger-worthy differences.

› **KRIS NERI**   Conflict is necessary in all fiction, but it's really the engine that drives crime fiction. Yet too many new writers avoid it, sometimes to the extent of putting the climatic scene off the page, when readers regard that scene especially as their payoff for having read the book. I don't have a writing tip for conflict as much as a life tip. I've noticed when people are not comfortable with conflict in their own lives, when they avoid asserting themselves—they're probably going to have a hard time writing it, and they'll give their characters their own excuses for avoiding it. If you're having trouble writing conflict, examine how you deal with it in your own life. Work through your issues, then take it to the page and make a deliberate effort to learn to deal with this troublesome element through your characters. If you have to force yourself to write it—do it. That teaches you to write conflict, and also you'll probably become more comfortable with it in your own life.

44. Writing a Few Chapters at a Time

If you only keep adding, little by little, it will soon become a big heap.—Hesiod

Now that you've outlined your book, drawn some characters, and have a sense of the dialogue, the process of writing chapters is a natural next step. You know that your story has certain goals. Maybe, you know how it will begin and how it will progress, and you have a pretty good idea of how it will end. As you write each chapter, you gain a sense of where you want to go next. Keep going, eventually closing chapters that will bring the story to a logical and exciting conclusion where everything will tie in.

> ROBERT GOLDSBOROUGH Most of my novels have been written in linear fashion—straight through from start to finish, and, at least in the early chapters, without my having a clear picture of the "twist" that is so important in the denouement of whodunits. But in two cases, at some point partway through the story, I suddenly saw how I could tie things up, so I immediately wrote the final chapter, out of sequence. Even today, I'm not sure which is the better way to attack a story. I'm inclined to believe it's a matter of personal preference for every writer—and for every story. I've known cases where authors write the end first.

> T.M. MURPHY I am very big on everything connecting in the end. I achieve this by reading what I am working on over and over again, making sure I have no throwaway lines. The other benefit of reading it continuously is that the book will reveal where it wants to go.

> MICHAEL BRACKEN I rarely plot an entire project in advance. I like to start with a strong opening scene—a hook—and then ask myself, "What happens next?" The process of discovery keeps me writing. I want to know what happens next, and the only way I'll know is to write the next scene.

> MICHAEL WIECEK I need the whole damn novel plotted out ahead of time, or I end up completely stuck in a lobster trap of dead-end plotlines and hopeless characters.

Of course, everyone has the experience of seeing some minor, overlooked character suddenly jump into the foreground and wrest the scene away from the protagonists. Usually these interlopers are funnier and more interesting than your carefully developed heroes. When that happens, you might as well hand them the reins for a while and see where you end up. Hopefully they'll stick more or less to schedule once granted their time in the sun. If they don't, maybe you're writing the wrong story. It's happened to me.

› **CARLY PHILLIPS**   Think ahead. Know not just where you are now but where you are going (even if you just envision it in your mind) and work toward a tangible goal.

45. Discovering the Ending

It is good to have an end to journey toward; but it is the journey that matters, in the end.—Ursula K. Le Guin

Few things could be more dissatisfying than investing time and money in a book that made promises that in the end it just couldn't keep. The ending was too contrived or too vague or there was no resolution. Whatever the reason, chances are, you won't read that author again because of the letdown. Think long and hard about your ending and how you are ultimately going to satisfy your readers. When readers get to your great ending, hopefully they are hooked on your work and hungry for your next novel. Then the only thing you'll have to worry about is all your fans who keep asking you again and again and again, "When's the next one coming out?"

› **WILLIAM LINK**   When lecturing at schools to fledging writers, I am invariably asked the same question, Should I know the ending of a mystery before I begin writing? There really is no answer here. I personally would say definitely, based on my own experience. We ran into terrible difficulties on *Columbo*, painting ourselves into a corner because we didn't have the final clue when we came to finale.

Contrary to this opinion is Robert B. Parker, who told me he never knows where he is going once he starts. Ditto for Elmore Leonard, and both men are masters of the genre. But I still think it's an easier ride if you know your destination.

> **JAMES F. MURPHY JR.** I really never have an ending in mind. I am optimistic that plot and character will lead me there. I don't want to write to a perceived ending because I feel that handcuffs me.

> **JOHN MCALEER** When I wrote my mystery novel, *Coign of Vantage, Or, The Boston Athenaeum Murders*, I knew how my protagonist, Austin Layman, would wrap everything up. But how it would actually end—the final sentence—was something I thought long and hard about. With the type of murder mystery I was writing, you want the reader to feel as if the world is a better place because of the protagonist's efforts, yet you don't want to preach either. My job was to entertain, but entertaining through murder is tough business. The object, I think, is to assure the reader that when the worst of all crimes is committed, justice will be served. I wanted to leave my readers with a feeling of hope, but I also didn't want them to think that my characters were done fighting crime. With that in mind, I decided to blend humor and subtext into my ending. I reassured the reader that for now all was well in Boston, but if needed, Austin Layman would be back on the case and ready to fight the forces of evil!

Part III

DISCIPLINE

When Edgar winner Joe Gores asked his college professor for advice on how to become a writer, he was told, "Go to a big city and rent a little room with a chair and a table in it. Put your typewriter on the table and your behind on the chair. Start typing. When you stand up ten years later, you'll be a writer."

One of the greatest lessons of discipline I ever learned was in Cub Scouts—not from the Cub Scout manual, but from my father, our den leader, during our group's annual campout. After a long day of blazing trails, foot races, and toasting marshmallows, we all settled into our tents for the evening and when the last flicker of flashlight-excitement finally came to an end, my father turned on his own flashlight when he thought I was asleep and began writing on a piece of paper he had brought. It wasn't a pad of paper or a notebook. Just a piece of paper. He and my mother were raising six kids at the time, each just one year apart, so money was often tight. To stretch every dollar, my father brought home scrap paper from Boston

College to prepare his rough drafts instead of buying notebooks. At the time, my father was writing Rex Stout's biography, and he had committed to completing at least one page a day—no excuses, not even a long day and night with high-adrenaline campers.

Rex Stout: A Biography would go on to unanimously win the Edgar Allan Poe Award in 1978 and presently—some three decades later—is in its sixth printing. When Little, Brown published the biography in 1977, the final page count came to 621 pages. I sometimes wonder which one of those pages my father wrote that night under the stars. Whichever page it was, it's in there somewhere doing its job.

Discipline is without a doubt one of the best qualities a writer can have—if not the best. All the creativity, mentoring, workshops, and cash advances in the world will not get your work on paper. Without the discipline to write and keep your schedule, your ideas may be lost forever.

Chapter 6

THE WRITING HABIT

46. Setting Reasonable Goals

You know, I just started writing and then I wrote every single day at the same time. I never have to make myself sit at the typewriter.
—David Sedaris

Businesses do it. Athletes do it. Students do it. Writers should too. Set reasonable goals. One of your first goals should be to write every day. Then the question becomes how much should you write? The answer is: as much as you reasonably can. Like anything, if you set the bar too high, you're going to knock it off, so be fair to yourself and your family. And remember, even some of the most successful authors are under the same time constraints you are. Most authors work, raise families, and have to find time to mow the lawn, scrape paint, and walk the dog.

For example, George V. Higgins's first novel, *The Friends of Eddie Coyle,* was published in 1972 while he worked full time at the U.S. Attorney's Office and raised a family. *Coyle* went on to become a bestseller and a blockbuster movie in 1974 starring Robert Mitchum and Peter Boyle. You might think that Higgins would be on easy street, but not so. A prolific writer, he stayed on at the U.S. Attorney's Office and practiced law privately well into the 1980s while teaching at Boston University and writing for several major newspapers. Another example, Mary Higgins Clark, was a single mother when she published her first major novel, *Where Are the Children*? Also, Dennis Lehane wrote his Shamus Award–winning novel, *A Drink Before the War*, (his first novel), in the front seat of his limo while waiting for his clients to return from their evening prowls.

Continuity will get the job done and get it done well. Making excuses that you do not have time will not.

› **JAMES M. CAIN**   I write every day, even if I intended to take a day off and relax. Promptly at 11:30, I go to work, and I work about four hours, or until I tire. Sometimes, I'm done in an hour, especially if the work goes well and I have two or three highs, spots where it really excites me. Highs are very exhausting, and if I quit at the end of an hour, it's really a good sign.

› **JAMES F. MURPHY JR.**   I set a goal of ten pages a day or four hours. I give myself a maximum of four straight hours and almost always that is continual writing.

› **S.J. ROZAN**   Write every day. *Every* day. But not like you're on a diet, where as soon as you goof up, you figure yourself for a miserable failure and give up, and you do this three times a year, with new and useless resolve each time.

No, write every day the way an athlete practices a sport, or a musician an instrument. You're doing the same thing: not just producing pages in your manuscript, but even more important, keeping fit, keeping toned, keeping in practice. Do this for the rest of your life. Or at least, the rest of your writer life.

47. Making Writing a Pleasure

Light tomorrow with today!—Elizabeth Barrett Browning

Write because you love to write. Because you need to write. Because you would be incomplete if you didn't.

Writing, editing, and rewriting can be physically and mentally tough work. Nevertheless, you shouldn't look at it from that perspective. Remind yourself why you are doing it—that your work will make other people happy, invite debate, or make readers once again believe in romance. It's okay to have a tough day where you have to slog it out in front of the computer, but overall, seek out the pleasure of writing, and readers will find pleasure and inspiration in your work.

› **SUZANNE BROCKMANN** I've frequently caught myself saying, "I have to write." Or, "I have to go finish that (expletive deleted) chapter."

Have to? *Have to* applies to school book reports or cleaning the bathroom. *Have to* infuses any task with a sense of unpleasantness. I *get* to write. I am *blessed* to be able to spend my days creating. I *need* to write the way I need food, sleep, and love, and often I need to write more than food and sleep. And yet, if I'm not careful, the use of one powerful word can change my gift to a chore.

› **JOANN ROSS** Writing isn't always easy. Sometimes it's flat-out hard. But, to paraphrase Tom Hanks, from *A League of Their Own*, it's *supposed* to be hard. If it wasn't hard, everyone would be doing it. That's what makes it great.

Fortunately, unlike in baseball, crying *is* allowed in writing. And whenever greeting people at Wal-Mart starts sounding like an appealing profession, I remind myself that people actually pay me to sit at home in my jammies and tell them stories. How cool is that?

> **JULIA LONDON**   Write with abandon; write with glee. Kick all the rules and boundaries out of your way, dive in, and swim for broke. The more you love what you are doing, the more your writing will shine.

> **SABRINA JEFFRIES**   Writing is only a pleasure when you're completely immersed in your story and it's going well. So don't expect it to be a pleasure when something's not right. Just do whatever it takes to fix it, even if it means a lot of hard work (redoing point of view, redefining a character, revisiting where your plot went wrong). Once you've located the problem, writing will become a pleasure again.

48. Writing Through the Blahs

Ninety-nine percent of the failures come from people who have the habit of making excuses.—George Washington

Whatever your daily writing goal is, stick to it even when you have the blahs. In fact, this might be the *best* time to write. Who can predict what creative juices might flow from your present state of mind. Moreover, writing when you feel a bit distressed might be the very thing to lift your spirits. Why not? After all, you write because you want to, and you want to because you enjoy it. So don't let the blahs distract you from your daily goal. Work through them and use them to your advantage.

> **JOANN ROSS**   When the writing gets tough, the tough keep writing. I've written with teenagers blasting video game aliens—with all the accompanying cheers and groans—on the

other side of a very thin wall. I've written at basketball practice, on planes, and sitting on a sidewalk curb waiting for the Fiesta Bowl parade to begin. Once I edited a manuscript during halftime at the Rose Bowl surrounded by tens of thousands of screaming fans. I've watched Nora Roberts madly typing away by the hotel pool at a conference, and let's not forget that Francis Scott Key wrote *The Star Spangled Banner* during a battle. Writers write. It's what we do.

> **SABRINA JEFFRIES** The best time to write is when your life is in the toilet. Writing offers an escape from your problems, so if you force yourself to write when you're in the doldrums, it will have the perverse effect of cheering you up. At the very least, it allows you to inflict your pain on your characters, which has the dual effect of giving them more depth while relieving your own tension.

> **BEVERLY BARTON** For some writers, being able to escape into their writing during difficult times is their salvation. Others cannot write a word and sometimes either a traumatic event or a series of difficulties can end a career. I've never had writer's block, even during some rough periods, but there have been times when I've had no choice but to take time off from writing to handle some of those curve balls life throws our way from time to time.

When you go through a rough patch—and you inevitably will—be kind to yourself. Cut yourself some slack. But don't use it as an excuse to stop writing. Give yourself whatever time you need to do whatever needs to be done, then force yourself back to the computer and write.

> **JULIA LONDON** The blahs suck. Words come like molasses, and they are usually monosyllabic. You feel like a hack and an ignorant one at that. You wonder why you ever thought you

could write anything more than a check. And even though each word you put down on paper will feel like another step uphill in deep snow, you must keep doing it until you reach your goal for the day. Tomorrow, you can go back and add some syllables and some genius. Tomorrow, you can breathe life into the molasses. But you cannot breathe life into a blank page.

49. Exercising Your Body

Even if you are on the right track, you will get run over if you just sit there.—Will Rogers

Different forms of physical activity enhance your creative juices. I enjoy mowing the lawn, gardening, and taking long walks.

Writers run the risk of leading very sedentary lifestyles. We have that nine-hour day at the office, the log-jam commute, and now we're adding to the "sit down" by spending extended time in front of the computer. We must find time for some kind of physical activity, not just for our bodies, but for our minds as well. You might think that exercise time is time away from writing, but it's not. When you exercise, the oxygen stimulates your brain, and this will help open your creative soul. Perhaps the next push-up you bang out will help you sort out a new idea. Great job. Now do another set!

> **HANK PHILLIPPI RYAN** Sleep is the first thing to go. Then exercise. And though that feels exciting at first, it's a dangerous precedent. I have a full-time job as an investigative reporter for a Boston television station. I used to think that was a 24/7 endeavor. Suddenly, I had to add writing novels. That was exciting and fulfilling, but where was the time going to come from? I had to learn to keep a balance—because if I got sick or burned out, I wouldn't be able to do anything well.

50. Finding Time to Recharge

Find a job you love and you will never work a day in your life.—Confucius

Everyone needs time to recharge their batteries. When I used to sand floors for a living, we would frequently run into an old house painter named Harold who insisted on taking a power nap each day after work in his office chair back at his shop. At the time, Harold was in his late sixties, and now, more than a decade later, I still see his van driving around town.

I'm not saying that you need to stop the presses every day at 4 P.M. to take a nap after cookies and milk, but try to find some time to relax each day, even if it is for only ten or fifteen minutes. Play your favorite CD, take a walk, go for a drive, fold laundry, get some sun, tend to your houseplants, or meditate. Refilling the tank will make you far more productive and creative.

Because writing is so solitary, it might be a good idea to make your relaxing activity something you do with your spouse, significant other, or pet. Take advantage of whatever it is that will help you recharge your batteries.

> **HANK PHILLIPPI RYAN** Making time for rest is an investment in your future, in your brain, in your creativity, in your stamina, and in your success. Some days, unless my impending deadline is unavoidably crushing, I say, I'm not writing today. I'm resting my brain. (Your brain is still working, of course, whether you know it or not. And sometimes it's coming up with wonderful stuff.) And I say, Today, I'm working out. Riding my bike. Walking through the garden.

> **ED GAFFNEY** When I need to recharge, I turn to one of three things: books that I love, movies or television shows that feature great writing, or the thesaurus.

Obviously, this kind of advice is entirely dependent on individual taste. For my money, there's nothing like J.D. Salinger's *Raise High the Roof Beam Carpenters*. But some of the descriptive passages from F. Scott Fitzgerald's *The Great Gatsby* also do the trick for me, and I also love Kaye Gibbons's *Ellen Foster*. All I have to do is read these things, and I want to write.

Other times, especially when it seems like I'm just not doing my best work, I take a stroll through my thesaurus to remind myself of the richness of our language. I make a list of words that catch my eye that I rarely use in my prose: fearsome and feckless, gumption and guise, prattle and precipitous. Even if the words never appear in anything I write, the process of writing them down seems to energize me.

› **BEVERLY BARTON** Take time off between books, the more time you can afford to take off the better. During this off time, I read for pleasure. And because I'm an old-movie aficionado, I'll often spend an entire day watching one movie after another. Just as we must eat to nourish our bodies, we must feed our minds. After writing a book, I feel mentally and emotionally depleted, as well as physically exhausted.

51. Getting A Good Night's Sleep

In the writing process, the more the story cooks, the better. The brain works for you even when you're at rest. I find dreams particularly useful. I myself think a great deal before I go to sleep, and the details unfold in the dream.—Doris Lessing

I think that many of us have been guilty of pulling all nighters whether it was for that troubling French exam, term paper, or keg party. As a creative writer, however, this is not a habit you want to get back into.

Researchers at Harvard Medical School conducted a study to determine under what circumstances people best come up with creative solutions. Their findings showed that people who had a good night's sleep doubled their creative abilities. So, if you're having trouble with that plot line, skip the keg party and hit the mattress. It's better to double your creativity than your aspirin intake.

> **ED GAFFNEY** I've had many instances of waking up after a good night's sleep with the answer to a question that had been bedeviling me the day before, such as how to increase the tension in one section of the book, how to create an effective relationship between a character and the reader without slowing down the pace of the narrative, and even how to end a book.

I strongly believe that those experiences were not coincidences. I believe that my subconscious mind was working while I was asleep.

> **STEPHANIE KAY BENDEL** A good night's sleep has another advantage. I pay attention to my dreams, and more than once they've inspired a successful story. One such tale, aptly called "Deathdream," involves a woman whose dreams come true. The trouble is that she is dreaming that her kind, loving husband is going to poison her. When she enlists the aid of a detective, the dream becomes more complicated: The detective is *helping* the husband to poison her! As complex as this plot seems, I actually dreamed almost the whole story one night! Ever since, I keep notes on my nocturnal machinations.

> **KIT EHRMAN** I'm sure getting a good night's sleep is helpful, but I've yet to experience it because writing wreaks major havoc with my sleep, especially when I'm plotting. I'm one of those writers who is always running to the computer in the middle of the night to jot down notes or even write a scene.

› MARY REED MCCALL   One of the classic images held dear by some people who ruminate on the lives of novelists is of the author toiling away in a garret (or alcove, basement, or any space removed a bit from the main part of a residence), with a single light/candle burning, as he or she pens challenging but ultimately perfect prose well into the wee hours of the night. While this is a romantic concept, it isn't necessarily productive in a creative sense. Nor, am I convinced, is the reality that spawned it rooted so much in author eccentricity as it is in the necessity for many writers to find some quiet, uninterrupted time during which to pursue their craft. What better time to be left alone to write than in the middle of the night, when virtually everyone else is wisely in bed?

I'll be the first to admit that I'm guilty of putting the stereotype into practice, sometimes writing until two, three, or even four o'clock in the morning. However, I'll also be the first to say that on many of those occasions, I might have been better off getting a (relatively) decent night's sleep before getting up and starting with fresh eyes and energy on my manuscript in progress.

Pushing onward when one is physically and perhaps mentally and emotionally exhausted has its place in many writers' lives (for example when a deadline is breathing down one's neck!), but there is something to be said for the fact that people think with more clarity, act and react to necessary changes more swiftly, and make fewer errors when we're rested.

So get a good night's sleep. Your body—and your manuscript—will thank you for it in the morning!

52. Making Your Health a Priority

If anything is sacred the human body is sacred.—Walt Whitman

As my dear mother used to advise when I turned my nose up at peas, "What you eat today is what you think tomorrow." And if that wasn't enough, my father would back her up with, "You don't live to eat, you eat to live!"

Take care of yourself and eat as healthily as you can. The stress of taking care of a family, dog, house, work, and the bills that keep multiplying is taxing enough. Now you have taken on the added stress of trying to write a book. Like raising children, parenting a book has its rewards, but it's not easy. Get every edge you can and hold onto it tightly. Vegetables will help strengthen your grip.

› **MICHAEL BRACKEN** While I would never be confused with a physical fitness freak, I've found that maintaining good health is important. I've changed my diet to incorporate more fruits and vegetables, and I reduced the amount of carbonated, caffeinated, and sugary drinks I consume. I keep two sets of handweights next to my chair—one set of eight-pound weights and one set of fifteen-pound weights—and I lift them during writing lulls.

› **JAMES F. MURPHY JR.** Health should be a top priority for a writer. Especially no alcohol—write clear-headed. I remember once I had *one* beer before writing, and it positively took that glorious edge off. The flow was gone.

Chapter 7

THE CHALLENGES

53. Writing Through Your Fears

I have always been pushed by the negative. The apparent failure of a play sends me back to my typewriter that very night, before the reviews are out.—Tennessee Williams

No one wants to write a bad book, page, or even sentence. We all want readers and critics to love our work. The reality is, we know that some people will not like our work, that not everyone will buy it, and that many reviewers won't even take the time to review it. These are not reasons to throw in the towel.

If we allow these fears to inhibit or preclude our writing, our dreams of writing are kaput before page one even gets off the ground. Put your fears behind you and get your novel written. Don't worry about making mistakes. Your novel can always be edited, even rewritten, just like almost every other novel is.

› **LORI AVOCATO** Dispel the fears that your work won't be good. It will be. Dispel the myth that you need the muse to strike. The muse is in your head. Always was. Always will be. You have total control. Dispel how your fingers tremble when you place them on the keyboard because you think you have nothing to write. You do. It's all inside of you. Type it out. You'll feel much better. Writers get crabby when they don't get those words out of their heads.

> **T.J. PERKINS**   Exactly what are you afraid of? Fear of failure? Fear that no one will like your story? This is where the old sayings "Buck up," "Grow thick skin," and "Let it bounce off your back" come in. It may sound harsh, but it really is true. I, for one, have felt the sting of rejection, for many years, and yes, I've grown thick skin and gotten tough. Because of those rejections, I found other avenues of penetrating the system to get what I want. I look at it this way: "No" just means they didn't understand the question.

54. Silencing Your Inner Critic

No matter how well you perform, there's always somebody of intelligent opinion who thinks it's lousy.—Sir Laurence Olivier

New York Times bestselling novelist David Sedaris came up with a great way to silence his inner critic. Before his blockbuster book *Me Talk Pretty One Day* was released, he convinced himself that the critics would pan it, so he came up with an ingenious way to beat them to the punch. Sedaris proceeded to write into his journal every bad review he could possibly think of. His philosophy was that no one else could possibly say anything worse about the book than he just did, so therefore, he could live with any scathing review that might come along. As a result, he was able to silence his inner critic. The critics could do nothing to him that he had not already done to himself.

It's okay to be critical and discriminating of your work. This self-analysis encourages us to strive toward our best. The trick is not to be so critical that you never get any work done.

If everyone was too critical of themselves, there would never be any books written, trains built, medicines discovered, or TV shows created. Incidentally, *Me Talk Pretty One Day* received almost unanimously rave reviews.

> **JAMES F. MURPHY JR.**   I think most writers have self-doubt and maybe the Irish even more (it's a cultural thing for me) so I have to overcome it by dwelling on my four published novels. I have to think positively.

> **ED GAFFNEY**   I silence my inner critic in different ways, depending on how he's acting.

If my inner critic is being rational (actually trying to help me write a better book), I generally can quiet him down by explaining that the best way for criticism to help produce better results is for it to take place at specified times in the writing process. My work does not improve by hearing from my critic as I'm trying to fall asleep, for example. I remind my inner critic that there will be plenty of time to give me his thoughts when I'm rereading what I wrote yesterday, or last week.

However, if my inner critic responds irrationally (and I've heard this described as "blank page syndrome" or "Shakespeare syndrome"—why bother even starting if your first line isn't as good as anything Shakespeare wrote?), my strategy changes. I do two things. First, I do not directly engage the enemy. I don't go one-on-one with the irrational inner critic. He always will win. There's always something that could be written better, someone who has achieved more success, or a line from Shakespeare that's better than the one I just wrote—I know these things. I don't need a nasty voice in my head to tell me so over and over.

Second, I ask myself, "What is the next sentence?" That's all I have to write, and it's good for me to remember it. And when I focus on that, my inner critic seems to drift away.

55. Dealing with Distractions

It matters if you just don't give up.—Stephen Hawking

When professional baseball players are batting, they concentrate on batting. When fielding, they focus on fielding. If you want to be a professional writer, you need to develop the same type of focus.

Don't let the concern of not knowing what comes next in your story deter you from today's work. It is natural to be concerned that you don't yet know how this story will end exactly or to worry that you may not be able to tie-in every loose end. You will overwhelm yourself and your work, however, if you spend too much time worrying about what comes next in your story.

Instead of concerning yourself with what comes tomorrow, be thankful that you have an idea today and that you have found time to get it down on paper. This does not mean that you should never plan for tomorrow's work. It just means that you should not let it control you to the point where it takes you away from what you are able to do today.

> **ED GAFFNEY** The way that I avoid distractions when I write is to do my day's writing before I do anything that could be seen as a distraction: before signing online to see what today's crazy politician/celebrity/sports star did, said, ate or drank, or which of them committed a felony; before checking e-mail, reading the newspaper, or peeking quickly at the television to verify that Meredith really is/isn't as good as Katie; before returning crazy Uncle Louie's phone call.

First thing in the morning, I shower, have breakfast, and sit down at the computer and write my pages. I know that all of the other stuff will still be there when I'm done, like a kind of reward for doing my work. (Except for Uncle Louie, who doesn't really count as a reward.)

In any event, I've found that by writing my pages before I do anything else each day, I am giving myself a consistent message that writing is my most important task. And it doesn't hurt that most days, I get my pages done, too.

› **CINDA WILLIAMS CHIMA**   Too many writers get involved in the business of marketing before they have a product to sell. Focus on craft. Nothing happens until you write the book. Once you've written the best book you possibly can, you can learn how to write a killer query letter, set up the website, and find yourself an agent.

Identify your prime writing time—the time of the day when brilliant ideas flow onto the page. Use it to write. Don't squander it working your day job, checking deal listings on Publisher's Marketplace, or Googling yourself.

56. Annihilating the Time Burglars

A little neglect may breed mischief: for want of a nail the shoe was lost; for want of a shoe the horse was lost; and for want of a horse the rider was lost.—Benjamin Franklin

Sometimes there is no way to avoid getting sidetracked when you're writing. You have to leave the phone on the hook because you're expecting a big call, the baby monitor has to be on, your neighbors have always been loud and guess what? They don't care if you need peace and quiet while you're trying to save old Hank Potter from the gallows! Somehow or another you will have to work around these distractions.

If we want to get our work done, we have to be honest with ourselves though and admit that some distractions are brought on by, well—ourselves. You have the power to eliminate many of them, so do so. When you sit down to start your daily goal, make sure that you have everything you need, so that you won't have to pop up and spend a half hour looking for that scrap of paper with your latest idea. Don't stop in mid-sentence to get up and make a cup of tea. (Okay, I'll admit it, I've done this myself.) Dust your computer screen after you get your work done. If your work for the day will require research, rather than surfing the net during your valuable writing time, do your research before you begin to write and have an idea of what you want to use from that research. This is something you could have pondered during that long commute this morning! All these things are time burglars, and they are the writer's arch enemy.

You may have only one hour a day, or maybe only a half hour, to accomplish your daily writing objective, so you must take full advantage of your actual writing time. Anticipate which time burglars might try to foil your productivity and annihilate them without mercy.

> **LIZ CARLYLE**   Many a road to deadline hell has been paved with painstaking research. Train yourself early on to separate minor research from your daily writing. They are not remotely similar processes. When you are writing, write. If you hit a point where some small bit of information is needed, mark it with an asterisk and move on. Perhaps you really do need to determine what sorts of neurotoxins were available to a homicidal herbalist in the sixteenth century. But you do not need it at precisely *that* moment—and if you break your flow, you'll be knee deep in the *Encyclopedia Britannica* for the next three hours. Wait. When you've got half a dozen of those pesky asterisks, set aside an hour or two for surfing the Net or perusing your library, and do them all at once.

> **JAMES F. MURPHY JR.**   To avoid wasting time, I force myself to the desk. Once I'm there, I'm off. I have a special place where

I write. If I can wrestle my old body to that place, I know I am there for only one reason—to write!

57. Making Sacrifices to Write

I am not a has-been. I'm a will be.—Lauren Bacall

How does one make time for anything nowadays? It ain't easy. The new writer's dilemma here though is obvious. You want to write a novel. You are going to write a novel. It will take lots of time. You will have to make sacrifices and somehow figure out a way to modify your daily itinerary.

Do you head out for work fifteen minutes early every morning because you want to pick up that cup of coffee from your favorite shop? Sounds like you could save fifteen minutes here. Do you head out to lunch with the boys everyday? This one may have to go, too. How about a morning break at work? Only ten minutes? Sounds to me like you could draft a good outline here for your daily quota. After all, you came up with a good idea during your commute, may as well get it down now. Your favorite program on TV? Gone. Strike all of these off your list of comfort times.

It sounds tough, indeed dire, but if there is one universal truth that new writers with families and full-time jobs share, it is that all of them were pressured to scavenge time that seemingly did not exist. I don't have much time to look back, but now, as I do, I can't even remember all the things that I had to sacrifice in order to write my first novels. Perhaps, in the end, they weren't that important, and I have my first, second, and third novels to replace them, and that's forever.

› **WILLIAM LINK**   Any free time you had is now writing time. Write everyday—no excuses. Even if it's only a quarter page of a novel or screen play, it keeps the fluids flowing.

> **JAMES F. MURPHY JR.**   I never can remember having to sacrifice because I have my priorities: my family and my teaching. Once my priorities are accomplished, I am free to write.

> **HANK PHILLIPPI RYAN**   I haven't had a vacation since—well, I can't even remember, but certainly not since I started writing mysteries. But I don't call it a sacrifice. I don't feel as if I'm giving up something; I feel as if I'm *getting* something. I love my work as an author, and some of the most precious time to me is the hours I spend creating my characters and their world. When you change your life for something you love, it doesn't feel like sacrifice. It feels like a gift.

58. Enjoying Times When You're "Not Writing"

Courage is very important. Like a muscle, it is strengthened by use.—Ruth Gordon

I remember when I first learned to drive, my mother threw me behind the wheel of her Chevy Chevette—a stick shift. "Left foot on the clutch. Hand on the wheel. Hand on the shift. Foot on the brake. Slide it into neutral! Don't stall when you get it into first." I stalled. And I stalled for a long time. How could I possibly remember all of these things let alone do them all?

But then, after weeks of practice, something amazing happened. I stopped thinking about driving. I took my head out of the equation, and my hands and feet took over. I was going from first gear to fourth gear without even thinking about it.

Writing isn't much different. When we take on daily chores or focus on our day jobs or our tasks in our lives, something amazing happens—ideas for our novels subconsciously begin to form and work their way to the surface. Before you know it, when you sit down at your computer or pull out a pen and paper, your fingers or pen begin to take over. You practiced, you put in the long hours. You had guts enough to get behind the wheel, and now you're on cruise control.

> **GREGORY MCDONALD**   I don't sit at a desk creating anything. I'm creating work while playing tennis, sailing, chopping wood, and fiddling with horses. I can't help it. By the time I sit at a desk, everything is pretty well written in my mind. What I do at a desk is editing, again and again.

> **ROBERT GOLDSBOROUGH**   I find that I'm thinking about my writing even when I'm away from my desk. I also suspect my subconscious is at work as well, because several times a plot idea or new development has suddenly dawned. This once happened in the middle of the night, and I went straight to the PC to set down what had come to me—as if in a dream.

> **JAMES F. MURPHY JR.**   I'm always writing when I'm not "writing," such as when I'm cutting the grass. When I drive to Boston College, I think of my writing course and with that coupled with the music of my CDs, my mind wanders creatively.

59. Overcoming Procrastination

Besides the noble art of getting things done, there is the noble art of leaving things undone. The wisdom of life consists in the elimination of nonessentials.—Lin Yutang

One of my favorite bits of advice comes from Ben Franklin. "Plough deep while sluggards sleep and you will have corn to sell and corn to keep." Franklin was, without doubt, one of the finest examples of nonprocrastinators. He was a true Renaissance man: author, inventor, newspaperman, politician, Constitutional architect, and exercise instructor. Franklin realized that wasted time is wasted creativity that can never be recovered. A writer's life has zero room for procrastination.

> **BEVERLY BARTON**   Procrastination is that little horned devil who sits on your shoulder and whispers in your ear, telling you about all the other things you need to do before you sit down and write. You need to do more research. You need to create a better outline from which to work. You should update your computer or printer. You need a new dictionary and/or thesaurus. You slept late this morning and are two hours off schedule, so maybe it would be better to start the book tomorrow.

Thankfully, there is an angel sitting on your other shoulder who is shouting, "Get to work. Now!" Listen to your angel. If writing is the way you make your living, you'll make yourself work. If you don't, you won't get paid.

> **T.J. PERKINS**   Procrastination is a huge monster for most of us to overcome. The only way I've found to avoid procrastination is to set a scheduled time, on particular days, when I was going to write *and stick to it*. Think of it as a job. You don't let running out with your friends, going to see a movie, or watching a show on TV keep you from your job, do you? Why should your writing time be any different? And remember, it is your special time, your personal time, your time to immerse yourself into the world you've created. So, why cheat yourself?

60. Facing the Blank Page

Even the highest towers begin from the ground.—Chinese saying

One of my colleagues on the Boston Authors Club told me of a writer he had met who confided in him that he was so petrified of the blank page that he would have to take a drink or two before he wrote. When I asked my friend if he recalled the writer's name, he thought for a moment and shook his head. Not surprising. Whoever this writer was, it is likely that he let his fears destroy his talents and perhaps even worse—him.

Don't let the blank page destroy you; let it redeploy you. If you can't think of anything to write today, shift gears and try to work on something else. My college creative writing professor would have us spend the first fifteen minutes of class "freewriting," writing the first things that came to our heads. Freewriting is a great way to stimulate the brain. If you practice freewriting, it eliminates the possibility of you ever facing a blank page again.

Think of the blank page as a new canvas upon which you are about to create something. The words you choose to put on this page can create a whole new world, story, chapter, setting, or character. You are in complete control. Look at this blank page as a fresh opportunity to create all of the new and wonderful ideas that no one else in the world can create except for you.

› **LORI AVOCATO**   You can fix, polish, and sell anything except a blank page. Ergo, sit down and write.

› **CINDA WILLIAMS CHIMA**   Don't end your writing session at the end of a chapter, or it will be more difficult to get started the next day. Stop in the midst of action.

› **LIZ CARLYLE**   Never look at a blank page for more than two minutes. Write something. Anything. Even garbage will get your neurons firing. Eventually it's apt to morph into something useful. If not, you can take pride in having resisted the urge to dawdle.

› **MICHAEL WIECEK**   Everyone's habits are different, but hardly any writer I know actually *likes* to sit down and open up a blank screen. In my case, it always takes about half an hour to start writing. Good days, bad days, inspired, uninspired—thirty minutes of undirected activity always seems to be necessary. Knowing that, I can force myself through it and then, most of the time, I'll come up to speed.

61. Overcoming Writer's Block

I can't understand the American literary block—as in Ralph Ellison or J.D. Salinger—unless it means that the blocked man isn't forced economically to write (as the English writer, lacking campuses and grants, usually is) and hence can afford the luxury of fearing the critics' pounce on a new work not as good as the last (or the first).—Anthony Burgess

Some authors contend that writer's block exists, and others flat out deny its force. Other authors don't know what to make of writer's block.

Mark Twain, for example, contended that after he wrote each book he would just simply have to wait until his tank filled back up again, yet he put *Adventures of Huckleberry Finn* aside for years because he didn't know how it would end. Regardless of what Twain really thought about writer's block, the fact is, he did complete *Huck Finn*, and it remains a major American novel.

If you are stumped, maybe you ought to put your project aside for a while and work on another. Keep your mind active and your creative juices flowing. By doing so, you give yourself a different perspective, just like the painter who examines her subject from all angles and depths. Try to think of writer's block as an opportunity to tackle another project or to gain the proper perspective on your present one.

> **LIZ CARLYLE** Writer's block exists only if you believe in it and grant it power over you. Adhere faithfully to your writing schedule. When it is time to sit down at the keyboard, sit.

> **RHYS BOWEN** Remember once you have created a character, it becomes that character's story, not yours. If you get writer's block, it could be because you're trying to force your character to do something he simply would not do, and he is digging his heels in.

> **GREGORY MCDONALD** To avoid writer's block, at the end of a writing day, regardless of how wiped-out you are, start the next day's work. Type a few sentences, even a few words. Even if what you noted is dead wrong, you've given yourself a place to start.

> **WILLIAM G. TAPPLY** Hemingway claimed he quit each day in the middle of a sentence. Another good way to prevent writing inertia is to leave off in the middle of a scene at the end of each session. The next time you sit down, a quick read of what you wrote the previous day will draw you back into the scene you were writing.

> **LORI AVOCATO** There is no such thing as writer's block. When I was a nurse, I could not go up to my boss and say, "You know, I just don't feel like doing any nursing today."

So, sit yourself in the chair and write. You'll be amazed at what good work comes out of your subconscious. (It's all in there to begin with!) Never accept the excuse that you "just don't feel like writing today."

> **ED GAFFNEY** Whenever I am stuck on a facet of a book I'm writing, I watch movies that I enjoy, that are somehow related to what I'm writing.

For me, the relationship between the movie and my writing doesn't have to be that strong. I recently wrote a legal thriller called *Enemy Combatant* about a lawyer who finds himself defending a man accused of the worse domestic terrorism attack since the Oklahoma City bombing. I saw it as a Hitchcock-like tale, so while I was writing it, I watched a few of my favorite Alfred Hitchcock movies with a similar feel—*Rear Window* and *The Man Who Knew Too Much*. Neither was a legal thriller, but each featured a sympathetic character struggling against overwhelming odds.

Similarly, when I was writing my first three books, which featured a pair of lawyers who were best friends, I found myself watching the Paul Newman and Robert Redford classics *Butch Cassidy and the Sundance Kid* and *The Sting*. Neither movie's plot was related to any of my books, but the expert depiction of the main characters' camaraderie put my brain into the right place.

› **CARRIE VAUGHN** Have writer's block strategies in place. Most professional writers will tell you that they don't get writer's block. They can't afford it when they have deadlines to meet and writing is their job. But I do get stumped at some point on most things I write. The following strategies work me through it.

Change location. If you've been writing on the computer at a desk, take a pen and notebook and go outside to write by hand for a while. If you write by hand, try moving to the computer for a while. Or sit on the sofa with a laptop.

Skip ahead. If a current scene is giving you trouble, skip to the next part where you know what happens. This will either give you a clearer idea of what needs to happen before that point, or it will illustrate that maybe you didn't need that scene in the first place.

Outline. I do this a lot. I sit down with pen and paper and brainstorm all the possible things that could happen at that point in the novel. That helps me figure out where I need to go and gets me writing again.

> **STEPHEN HARRIGAN**   For me, writer's block is nothing more than an information deficit. Through the years, I've noticed that whenever I hit a wall while I'm writing a book, the problem very rarely has anything to do with the writing itself. Sure, I deliberate over word choice, sentence structure, and metaphors, but that sort of tinkering is part of the joy of creative work and is not in itself anxiety-provoking. What leads to despair is a creeping realization that I don't really know what I'm writing about. If I don't know sufficiently well the world I'm trying to portray or the characters that inhabit it, the only cure is to actively search out knowledge through reading, traveling, and consulting with experts in whatever period and place I'm dealing with. This sort of intensive research, in addition to being a pleasure, almost always restores my confidence and points the way ahead.

62. Sticking with It

A novel is something that has to be endured by the writer. Anybody who can't go back for the fourteenth and fifteenth revision with freshness and enthusiasm ought to get out of the business.
—James M. Cain

When aspiring to be a novelist, the story of the tortoise and the hare is a good one to keep in mind. Getting a book written and revised can take years, getting an agent can take years, and getting your book on the shelf and creating a readership can take still more years. Make no doubt, the writing business is for people who are prepared for the slow and steady fight.

It's true that you can write a blockbuster novel and receive overnight success, but that is not the norm—far from it. And if that is what you are banking your career on, you have the hare's mentality. When it comes to writing, slow and steady wins the publishing contract. Don't give up. Keep pushing along, and you will get there.

> **MARY HIGGINS CLARK**   Stay with it. There is surely no sweeter satisfaction to the suspense writer than to hear a heavy-eyed friend say accusingly, "You kept me up half the night reading your darn book!"

> **CINDA WILLIAMS CHIMA**   Do give up. More readers for me. But seriously, stick with it. If you were going to be a brain surgeon, you would take the time to learn your craft. The same applies to writing. A teenager once asked me if I thought it was hard for teen writers to get published. I told her that, all things being equal, it was no more difficult for good teen writers to be published than for adults. But it's uncommon for teen writers to be good enough, because they haven't had time to hone their craft.

> **MARY REED MCCALL**   Aside from perfecting craft, persistence is probably one of the most important attributes a writer can cultivate. Before I was published, I remember hearing a speaker at a conference say something to the effect of, "You are only in control of one thing, when it comes to your writing career: writing the very best book you can, every time. Aside from that, it's all about luck and timing."

Persist. Don't give up. Use your talents, maximize your strengths, and challenge yourself to produce the best writing you possibly can each time you write . . . and then, when you've written it and sent it out into the world, be patient. Believe in yourself and don't give up because the next desk your manuscript lands upon might belong to the agent or editor who will fall in love with your voice, your vision, and your story. And I promise you when that happens, the wait will have been worth it.

> **HANK PHILLIPPI RYAN**   When I was in the midst of writing my first novel, *Prime Time*, I hit 40,000 words—about halfway through. I called my mother and said, "Wow, this is more difficult than I predicted. I hope I can finish it." My mother paused, with one of those patented mother-like pauses, and then she said, "You will if you want to."

I think about that every day. Of course, the publishing world is full of chaos, whim, and things we can't control. But you can control yourself. Do your best. Keep going. Meet your goals. Do you want to? You can.

63. Meeting Deadlines

The only limit to our realization of tomorrow will be our doubts of today. Let us move forward with strong and active faith.
—Franklin Delano Roosevelt

Philip E. Humbert, PhD, a motivator and editor of the popular newsletter *HABITs*, offers this great advice when it comes to motivation, "Create a map for getting there. And put dates on it! A goal to retire at age forty has no meaning without a savings and investment strategy. A goal to create your own business is just a fantasy without a plan to attract investors, find a location, hire staff, and sell your goods or services. . . ."

By setting deadlines, you are telling yourself that you are required to do something by a specific time and that no one else is responsible for fulfilling that obligation but you. Also, don't leave it to an agent, editor, or publisher to create the deadline. Make your own—and make it realistic. If you miss a deadline, don't throw in the towel. Things happen. If you did everything you could to meet your deadline, keep moving forward and finish the task as best you can.

> **CARRIE VAUGHN**   Respect deadlines!

> **JOHNNY D. BOGGS**   I believe in deadlines and never want to tick off my agent or publisher by being late.

> **MICHAEL WIECEK**   Keep your deadlines. No, really. Everyone nods their heads when this comes up, and yet somehow most everything runs late, creating headaches all around. Stand out from the crowd: Be on time.

> **TOM SAWYER**   Deadlines should be right up there with Mom's apple pie. Setting a minimum daily word or page count goal for yourself is *essential*. And speaking of mothers, their penchant for laying guilt on us can be a great motivator. Mine comes late every afternoon in the form of a ghostly voice repeating a number done on me from about age five: "Tommy, you're *not* living up to your potential."

> **ROBIN MOORE**   Don't miss a deadline, especially the deadline to turn in the title for your book. If you have a good title, fight for it, and get it to your editor on time. Your book is counting on you! The original title Little, Brown wanted to give *The French Connection* was *The Patsy Fuca Case*. I had made the mistake of not giving Little, Brown a title and when I finally came up with *The French Connection*, they said that it was too late because *The Patsy Fuca Case* covers had already been printed, and they didn't want to incur further costs. I made a case for *The French Connection*, and finally the executives agreed on the new title. I promised never to be late again on a cover title, and I haven't!

64. Coping with Rejection

My favorite rejection letter was from an agent who said, "We don't have time to take on any new clients, and if we did, we wouldn't want you." But I kept trying. My second book got published. The first one never did.—Lisa Scottoline

Rejection is part of the process, so get used to it. Rejection letters are not fun, and they can shatter your confidence, but only if you let them. In fact, if you are clever and industrious, you can use rejection letters to your advantage.

Most of the rejections I receive are standard formatted ones that are probably photocopied a hundred times and sent out in bulk. I keep those rejections in my desk drawer as inspiration. They are fuel to feed the fire.

Every so often, however, I receive a personal rejection that may even comment on my work. In these instances, I send the agent a thank you letter for taking the time to read my work and offer comment. As a result, one agent wrote me back and invited me to resubmit my work or any other work I had. I heavily revised the manuscript I had sent him, and although he liked it, he again rejected it with some thoughtful remarks, but he did not invite me to resubmit. I took the hint and heavily revised the manuscript again and submitted my synopsis to another agent. He e-mailed me the next day asking for the first thirty pages. I sent them along, and one week later he asked for the whole manuscript. One week later, I signed a contract with him.

Rejections are what you make of them. They can wound, but they can't kill if you don't let them. And when you recover from your wounds, you will be stronger, wiser, and more determined.

> **CARLY PHILLIPS** You'll experience lots of rejection on the way to publication and even later on from readers and reviewers. Just know that one person's opinion isn't fact.

> ROBIN MOORE   My book *The Green Berets* was rejected mercilessly. That was about fifty books, four million copies sold, and one major motion picture ago. One closed door opens another. And remember that old maxim that professional writers are just amateurs who never quit.

> MICHAEL BRACKEN   A writing career is nothing more than a long series of disappointments punctuated by occasional moments of success. One of the most difficult lessons I learned was that rejection is rarely personal. Just because a manuscript is returned by one editor doesn't mean there's anything wrong with the manuscript. The only way to know is to put the manuscript right back in the mail and to continue submitting the manuscript until all reasonable markets have been exhausted. Maintaining a long writing career involves a little bit of talent, a little bit of luck, and a great deal of determination.

> MARY REED MCCALL   Rejections can be horribly discouraging. I accumulated my share of them, but I was also fortunate that I had a stubborn streak when it came to my writing. When I'd receive a rejection letter, I'd allow myself to feel lousy for a bit, then I'd vent and get indignant at the rejecting agent or editor for his/her lack of vision. Then I'd remind myself that this latest rejection was for the best because the only agent or editor I wanted working with me and my book was one who was in love with my writing and my story. I wasn't going to settle for anything less. And I didn't.

> SUZANNE BROCKMANN   One of my earliest rejection letters described both my book and my writing as being "too gritty" for the romance genre. Instead of changing my style and trying to jam myself into the standard mold, I searched for and found a publisher and an editor who liked me just the way I was.

Years later, I started getting reviewed, and to my amusement the word "gritty" often came up, but always in a positive way. "Gritty and realistic, Brockmann's books stand out in the crowd."

My perceived flaw has become my winning strength.

> **BILL PRONZINI** Don't allow rejections to bother you. Every professional author has been rejected one time or another. Many novels, including such mega bestsellers as *Love Story* and *Jonathan Livingston Seagull*, received numerous rejections before they were finally published. It only takes one editor to like a given manuscript enough to buy it.

> **JENNIFER BLAKE** Here's my three-step program for coping with rejection.

Start on something new the instant a finished project goes out the door. Blighted hope doesn't hurt as much if you're excited about the next story.

Never accept one editor's opinion. They may have bought a similar story last week; just published something closely related; be biased against your style, title, POV, or subject matter; have read your manuscript in the middle of a personal or work-related crisis; or had their acquisition budget slashed so they aren't buying anything. A thousand reasons for rejection exist, none of them necessarily a considered judgment of your work. Send it out again. If you must abandon a project, remember it's just one idea. The great joy of writing is that there are a billion more out there. Write something new, write something different, write something better.

> **ROBIN MOORE** When I returned home from Vietnam, no one would publish my account of the war. In fact, my initial publisher backed out of the deal. Then, ten major publish-

ers rejected my book. They rejected it because it was a factual account. I redeployed, converting the book into fiction by simply disguising the names and locations. Finally, the book was accepted by Crown Publishers, but with only a modest 2,500 book run. And that's all it took. The novel I'm talking about is *The Green Berets*, which went on to sell more than four million copies, was made into a major motion film staring John Wayne, and is still in print more than forty years after its release.

65. Not Being Afraid to Fail

If I had to live my life again, I'd make the same mistakes, only sooner.—Tallulah Bankhead

There is a story about a woman who said that when she was in grammar school, she was always dying to go to middle school. Then, when she was in middle school, she was dying to go to high school, and in high school she was dying to go to college and then dying to have a family and then dying to retire. Then one day she woke up and realized that she was dying. She had wished her life away.

We can do this with our dreams: wish them away or let them slip away because we are afraid to fail or afraid to get started because we are waiting for the right moment. As a writer, you can be sure of one thing: You will experience failures. Not all the time, but you will. A story you love and cherish will get rejected, or worse there will be no market for it.

One of my colleagues on the Boston Authors Club told me that she was talking to a writer who had been nominated for the Pulitzer Prize. My friend told the writer that it must be great to have everything accepted now that you have been nominated for a Pulitzer. The writer said that she wished that was the case, but it wasn't. She still received rejections for her work.

If you stick with writing, you will have successes and failures. But you will only fail in perpetuity if you never take the chance. Don't let your dreams slip off into old age and die.

› **T.M. MURPHY**   Everyone fails in this business. The biggest thing you have to remember is never lose confidence in your own ability. If you believe in yourself and your book, nothing anyone says or writes will stop you from achieving success. I always keep in mind that Michael Jordan was cut from his basketball team in junior high school. Did that stop him? Tom Brady was a sixth round draft choice, and Dr. Seuss's art teacher told him he had no talent. Always believe in yourself!

Chapter 8

THE EDITING PROCESS

66. Completing Your First Draft

You have to expect things of yourselves before you can do them.—Michael Jordan

When I first began practicing law, I met with an old gentleman who wanted me to write his will. I was still wet behind the ears, and I admitted that I didn't know a will from an affidavit. "Don't worry if you make a mistake," he told me. "Sometimes your mistakes help you." What he was telling me was to take a chance, and he was right. You won't get anywhere if you don't take some chances. I don't go out of my way to make mistakes, but I have to say that the old gentleman was correct that sometimes they do help us.

Keep this mind when you write your first draft. Don't worry if you make mistakes, or what you think might be mistakes. Your first draft will take your mind and characters places you never dreamed of, and some of the mistakes you make will serve you well throughout your career as a novelist. The mistakes that don't serve you well, you can correct. After all, it is better to have a terrible first draft than no first draft at all.

> **CINDA WILLIAMS CHIMA**   Be willing to write a bad first draft if that's what it takes to finish. Once you have something down on paper, you can fix it, but you need something to work with.

> **MARY HIGGINS CLARK**   I know too many people who've spent months working over the first chapters of their projected novels. That's wrong. Get it down. Bumble it through. Tell the story. When you have fifty or 100 pages typed, you've got something to work with.

> **ED GAFFNEY**   Carefully examine the phrase "first draft." There's a reason the word "first" is in there. It strongly implies that there's going to be a second draft. And if you write anything like me, there's going to be a third.

And a fourth.

And probably a fifth.

In fact, my last novel had twelve drafts. Now that's not to say that I wrote a completely different version of the book, cover to cover, twelve times over. But I can tell you with great assurance that my first draft was significantly different than what ended up appearing on bookstore shelves.

In fact, the first draft of my first book, *Premeditated Murder*, was substantially different from the "final" version that was accepted by my publisher. And that accepted version was then dramatically revised before publication.

So was the first draft of my first book a bad first draft? I guess so. It certainly was bad if you compare it to the final, published effort. But it was a good thing that I wrote that bad first draft. If I hadn't, I never would have gotten published.

67. Editing and Rewriting

The only true creative aspect of (novel) writing is the first draft. That's when it's coming straight from your head and your heart, a direct tapping of the unconscious. The rest is donkey work. It is, however, donkey work that must be done . . . you must rewrite.
—Evan Hunter (Ed McBain)

Authors' opinions vary when it comes to when you should revise your draft. Some insist that you write the whole draft through without looking back, and others advise that you revise as you go. What to do?

First, consider which approach is more likely to get you to finish your first draft. As I've stated again and again, the most important objective is to get your novel written. If you don't, you have nothing to work with.

Let's consider what the "don't look back philosophy" has to offer on this point. By not backtracking each day, you are always moving forward, getting closer and closer to the last page where you finally type "end." The beauty here is that because you have a full manuscript, you can print it and begin to edit, research, and build continuity and structure in your novel as a whole rather than piecemeal. If you had edited as you went along, you might still be stuck on page fifty!

Sounds like the perfect way to write, but wait a minute, we need to hear from the "edit as you go" camp." It's a wonderful, triumphant feeling when you get that page or chapter for the day completed, print it, and then reread your creations later that afternoon or evening before you go to bed. Here you can jot down some edits, form new ideas, or discover opportunities for character development. Another advantage to editing as you write is that daily you reinforce exactly what is happening in your story. When you begin writing the next day, you'll know exactly where you left off yesterday and perhaps have a better idea of where the story is going. And maybe you'll head off a few plot glitches. In the end, whether you edit or not on a daily basis will be up to you. Try both ways and see which you feel comfortable with.

> **LORI AVOCATO** Write that first draft all the way through without looking back! Get that internal editor off your shoulder if you are the type of writer who keeps polishing the first three chapters—and doesn't finish the work. The first draft is all creative stuff that comes to us, often as a surprise. There's nothing like reading what you wrote and mumbling, "Wow. I wrote that!" Let your stream of consciousness flow, and the words will appear on your monitor. You will often be amazed at how damn good they are! And then someone will buy your words, and that is a good thing.

> **VICKI STIEFEL** First-draft rule: Don't go back. I love to edit. Love it! So when I'm writing a first draft of a new novel, I never do it. What! Yup, I never go back and edit. Why? If I did, I'd end up with about twenty pages of really, really, really well-edited material. And that would be it. On a first draft, I push forward. Period. *Gee, but I'd love to go back and just tweak that one small section.* Nope, not allowed. I push forward. *Golly, if only I could smooth out those pages. I know they'd be better.* Probably right, but no way, not now. *Gosh, it would be great if I could have these words in the "real" Portuguese right now. I'll begin that research and . . .* Forbidden. Don't do it. Just jot some quick notes and move on. Move forward. Always forward. Relentlessly forward. And that's how I write some 400-plus manuscript pages for a novel.

Side roads are great, if you're driving a car or taking a hike. For me, they're crummy when writing a novel. So I write on, and write on, and write on. And, suddenly, I'm there. Whew.

And when I've finally made it to the finish line, I smile. Because that's when I pull out my pen, and I edit, edit, edit the bahoosie out of the manuscript. That's when I do thorough and important research. That's when I check spelling, continuity, and a million other things. But not before then. Because if I did, I'd never have finished book one.

> **CYNTHIA RIGGS** Don't edit as you write. According to right brain/left brain students, your right brain allows you to dash off stuff uncritically. Let the right brain help you get a chapter or so written, then at a different time, let your left brain loose to edit. One cause of writer's block may be the warring of the two sides of your brain, where you write three or four words, then examine those three or four words critically.

> **JOHNNY D. BOGGS** If something stops me during the writing or proofreading process, it's likely going to stop the reader. So that means revision, editing, tightening, deleting. I keep focused on the story. What I'm writing, even if it's dialogue, has to move the story forward. If it doesn't do that, I have more work to do.

> **CINDA WILLIAMS CHIMA** Don't be afraid to rewrite if you have to. It's very freeing to find out you can do major surgery on a novel and not ruin it. You may even improve it. I found out through the editing process that I could rewrite the beginning and the ending, change the gender of the villain, get rid of the dad who had nothing to do, move the action to the city, and cut fifty pages without ending up with blood on my hands.

> **JAMES M. CAIN** I rewrite so much I lose track of how many drafts it takes to finish a book—at least four or five, sometimes more.

› **KIT EHRMAN**   When I sat down to write *At Risk*, I was essentially teaching myself to write. I jokingly referred to the undertaking as "the first thing I've written since ninth grade Creative Writing that's more complicated than a grocery list." Not surprisingly, that first draft was a huge, unwieldy thing.

But I was not discouraged. I kept editing. I wasn't in a rush. I didn't have a deadline, I enjoyed the process, and I'm a stubborn person. When many writers might have shoved that manuscript under the bed or buried it deep within a desk drawer after the fifth or sixth edit (and started book number two) I combed through it with renewed enthusiasm, even after a writer whom I admire told me the story had no plot! My protagonist became more proactive, the plot more tightly woven. I embedded subtle clues and red-herrings throughout the narrative as I became more adept at plotting a mystery.

I must have edited *At Risk* more than twenty times. I could flip open the manuscript, glance at a line or two, and know exactly which scene I was looking at. But what those early edits consisted of was *cutting*. I learned to embrace that often repeated mantra that every scene must move the story forward or, at the very least, define character. If I could not justify a scene, it was gone. I got over the trauma of cutting—words, phrases, sentences, paragraphs, scenes, and (gulp!) chapters, and I eventually ended with a lean but complicated mystery.

Needless to say, this was no easy task. But I discovered a way that made it less painful. I created a "Cuts" document. Everything I cut went into that separate file. Nothing was ever *gone*. If I changed my mind, I could reinsert it with the click of a mouse.

As I matured as a writer, the "Cuts" documents for each book shrunk because I was evaluating scenes *before* I wrote them. The "Cuts" document for *At Risk* is 190 double-spaced pages. For *Triple Cross*, it's seven.

Around edit number ten of *At Risk*, I realized I needed to do a major story revamp, so I copied the entire manuscript into another document for safekeeping. This freed me to be as bold and daring as I liked. If I messed up in the revision, I still had the earlier version to fall back on. This is a nice strategy for short stories, too.

68. Asking for Feedback

Everyone needs to be valued. Everyone has the potential to give something back.—Diana, Princess of Wales

When it comes to writing a novel, you sometimes have to look at your work as a business, and like most businesses you will likely need help running it. You may need help with research, grammar, plot structure, dialogue—whatever it takes to get the job done efficiently.

For example, when my father, John McAleer, wrote *Unit Pride*, several scenes took place in Japan where a couple of American GIs were on R&R. Because these soldiers would be spending U.S. dollars in Japan, my father wanted to know what the rate of exchange was back in the early fifties. This was long before the Internet, and while my father probably could have tracked down the information here in the United States, a friend of his happened to be traveling to Japan. My father asked if he could find out the information for him while he was in Japan. The friend was delighted to help. Later, a reader wrote my father, complimenting him on his research with respect to the Japanese rate of exchange. When my father showed the letter to his friend who helped him, his friend was equally as delighted and really felt that he was able to contribute.

You will find that most friends and colleagues want to help you with your book, so if help is offered and you can use it, take it. One way your friends and family may be especially eager to help is to review your book for you before you send it off to your agent or editor. Ask for feedback from people you respect who are willing to give it freely.

> **WILLIAM G. TAPPLY** A trusted critic—someone who will read your work objectively and critically and will tell you the hard truth—is worth her weight in royalty checks. Nurture her and love her and buy her flowers.

> **CINDA WILLIAMS CHIMA** Positive feedback doesn't make you a better writer, but it can give you the strength to go on. Any critique of a work should begin with what's working. However, it can be risky to seek feedback on your work too soon. Early critique can kill your momentum. Sometimes it's best to get your first draft completed before you begin to edit in earnest.

> **JAMES F. MURPHY JR.** The only recruit I have is my son, who is a writer. I do not share ideas with others because once the writer talks about what he or she is writing, the glow, the energy, the excitement is lost.

> **KIT EHRMAN** Once I got busy writing Steve Cline's latest adventure, *Triple Cross*, my husband would find a printout of each immerging chapter on his computer keyboard because he's my first reader. I relied on him for "reader response" and for detecting logic problems I couldn't see because I was too close to the story.

I also relied on fellow Poisoned Pen Press author Beverle Graves Myers, creator of a beautifully written Baroque Mystery Series set in the declining days of the Venetian Empire. We've fallen into a pattern of exchanging chapters for critique that works well for both of us.

Once I finished the manuscript, I shared it with my sister, my mother, and a few select friends whom I trust to give me honest feedback. Well, I don't really expect negative feedback from my mom, but I don't want her feeling left out.

> **JO BEVERLY** Get some feedback. It needn't be a critique group or even another writer, unless that suits your creativity. To me, it's important to hear the echo from the other end. We write from within ourselves, creating a certain reality, but we have no idea what reality we've created until someone echoes it back to us. We might hear back a "cling" when we thought we'd sent a "clang."

I don't think we can rely entirely on agents and editors for this, for they have their own tastes, but above all their own concerns, which may not be those of our readers. Yet our readers in the end decide if we live or die.

> **HANK PHILLIPPI RYAN** Though my friends may clamor to see it, I don't show my work in progress to them. Also, I don't have a writing group. It's not that I don't care what my pals and colleagues think or that I don't respect their opinions or want their input. I do. But not while I'm in the process of creating my book's world. Everyone has an opinion, or an idea—and although I may be depriving myself of valuable input, I may be too easily detoured from the path I'm trying to create.

I do rely on friends for understanding and patience. When everyone is out at the pool or the movies or at the beach or skiing, and I'm home typing away, I know I can count on their support and enthusiasm, and that's critically important.

69. Letting Your Manuscript Steep

Delay is preferable to error.—Thomas Jefferson

Each month, I meet with my colleagues from the New England Chapter of Mystery Writers of America. After our monthly meeting not too long ago, we went out for dinner and talked about what we normally talk about—writing. Not surprisingly, we don't always come to the same conclusions on such subjects, but on this particular night one of our colleagues got on to the subject of when a manuscript is ready to submit to an agent or editor. While we came to no real conclusion on this subject other than, "Well, it's never going to be perfect, so you have to send it at some point," we did all agree that more often than not new authors send out their manuscripts too early, long before they are edited and revised properly. This can be a fatal mistake for aspiring authors.

Few things are worse in an author's life than blowing a promising lead with an agent or editor by sending them a manuscript that isn't ready for publication. The book will be rejected, and any good will you had will be lost.

So let your manuscript steep. Edit it, revise it, let trusted friends and writing group members read it, and then put it aside for a while, maybe a month or so. Then pick it up and read it with a fresh set of eyes and from a new perspective. More often than not, you will be glad you didn't send it out prematurely and lose a good lead.

› **CARLY PHILLIPS** Revision is your friend. Don't get frustrated by having to fix things. Just don't get hung up fixing so you never finish the book!

› **BEVERLY BARTON** The best advice I was ever given about preparing your manuscript to send off to an editor was this:

After you finish the book, read/proof it twice, then mail it off. If you proof it more than twice, you run the risk of polishing all the original creativity out of the story.

If you're not under contract (don't have a deadline), let the manuscript sit for a week or two, then polish/proof it one final time before sending it. However, writers under contract, with one deadline after another, seldom have that luxury.

No matter how many times you revise and polish, in the end, the book will never be as good as you had hoped it would be. I think for most writers, the reality never equals the dream.

70. Writing a Pitch Synopsis

I can't write a book commensurate with Shakespeare, but I can write a book by me.—Sir Walter Raleigh

The purpose of a pitch synopsis is to tell people succinctly what your book is about. Some writers write them, but others don't. I like them because they give me a feeling of preparedness.

Another good reason to have a pitch synopsis is so down the line when your book gets published, you can give it to your publicist, who will want to know briefly what your book is about. Thanks to your preparation with your pitch synopsis, your work is already done, and your book is ready to promote.

When writing fiction, I will draft a long synopsis and a short synopsis. My long synopsis will include the usual suspects: outline of the story, main characters, chapter summaries, and conclusion. This type of synopsis is long and difficult to write.

My short synopsis will be 100 to 150 words, and I draft this after I have written the book. Here is where I use all my great thrill words such as double-cross, horrific murder, no way out! I call this my pitch synopsis, and I use it to send to agents, editors, or authors from whom I'm asking a blurb.

Writing a pitch synopsis takes practice, but I find it to be incredibly fun. I enjoy finding ways to distill my entire novel down to just a few words. I think the best way to do it is to read flyleaf after flyleaf and movie synopsis after movie synopsis. You want to develop a voice for this style of writing. Learn what type of words attract you to books and movies and how you can use them for your books.

> **MICHAEL WIECEK**   I hate synopses, and I've never managed to write one. How the hell can you boil down a novel from 400 pages to three?

And what does the reader of a synopsis expect to learn from it, anyway? I'm not nearly good enough a writer to convey tone, voice, and character and summarize a 90,000-word plot in five paragraphs. Someone who writes in romance told me that the synopsis is used to prove you understand the expectations of the genre. Well, okay, I guess. But I've never heard another good reason, and even that sounds weak to me.

If the demand for a synopsis is nonnegotiable, do the best you can. Otherwise, just skip it—attach Chapter One, or a list of writing credits, instead. For me, the whole point of the game is to get them to read the first few pages. After that, it's all about the writing, as it should be.

> **JOAN JOHNSTON**   What is the importance of crafting a synopsis? A synopsis should be a short story of the book—in the present tense. It should tell who the main characters are and describe them, and it should tell what the major conflict is and how it will be resolved. A synopsis can be one paragraph or sixty pages—however much the author needs to be able to write the book.

For most of my career, I've written 20-page synopses for 400-page books. Once I've written a synopsis, *I never look at it again!* A synopsis is only a guide for you, to give you an indication which direction you want to go. The characters will write the book. Trust me, they will.

Having said that, as a commercial fiction author who needs to write two books a year, I don't let my characters run too far afield from where I want them to end up—based on my synopsis. Otherwise, I'm going to need to throw away forty or fifty pages during which the characters went off on a tangent. The problem a lot of writers have is once they've written those pages, they hate to throw them away, and they may end up with a book that meanders its way from the start to the finish.

71. Asking Other Authors for Blurbs

Let any man speak long enough, he will get believers.
—Robert Louis Stevenson

I was at a book signing once for Sue Grafton, a wonderfully talented mystery writer. Although it was a hot summer night and the line wrapped around the street, by the time I reached Grafton, she was still very pleasant after signing what must have been hundreds of books. I had a number of first editions, and I confessed to her that they were my mother's, who wanted to be here tonight, but couldn't because she was sick. Grafton immediately pulled out a card and wrote down her personal address and told me that if my mother wanted any signed labels for her other books, she should just write her.

Grafton is just one of the many wonderful and generous writers that I have met through the years. This type of generosity has given me the courage to write established authors and ask for help.

You may wonder when you read the back of a book how this new author obtained such a nice blurb from such an established author. Chances are, the new author just asked. My approach has always been this. When I write an author, I explain who I am and then state straight out that I would like to ask a favor. I don't beat around the bush. I don't hint that I would like a blurb. I ask for one, but I explain that I realize his time is valuable and if he doesn't have the time I truly understand. Then I ask him if I can send my one-page synopsis (pitch synopsis) or first chapter for their consideration. If you ask an author if you can send your full manuscript, you can just imagine how overwhelmed he would feel. It's better that you offer him a glimpse of your work, just enough to give an understanding of your writing style and what the story is about. He can ask for more if he wants to author a blurb for you. This has been my system, and although it hasn't always been successful, I have obtained some wonderful blurbs and encouragement over the years. And when authors have turned me down, they have invariably thanked me for my understanding of their busy schedules.

Advance praise is not absolutely necessary, but if you can get it, get it. By obtaining blurbs, you draw more notice with agents and, therefore, publishers because you have enhanced the marketing potential of your work.

72. Sending Off Your Manuscript

The secret is not to try to be perfect. If you try to be perfect, you procrastinate, you go over and over what you wrote, you make no forward motion. Trying to be perfect doesn't produce masterpieces, only agony and slow writing.—Stephen J. Cannell

Once your manuscript is complete, you're ready to send it off to your agent to review, or to many agents to try to find one to represent you. The catch is, rarely will an author feel that her manuscript is 100 percent ready to make the rounds to agents.

At some point, however, you must send your manuscript out if you ever expect to be published. But even though you have doubts about your work, despite the editing, feedback, and re-editing, you do have control over many things to show an agent that you are the real McCoy.

When you submit your manuscript, make sure that you follow the agent's specific guidelines for submission exactly and provide a self-addressed, stamped envelope for a response. By respecting your submission and showing that you respect the time and energy of the professional you are sending it to, you are letting the agent know that you are a professional, too.

Additionally, show the agent that your ideas are fresh and contemporary and that you're not trying to sell her some shop-worn idea. Proper submissions, a new voice, and a consistently structured manuscript will increase your odds of an objective reading and therefore, a better chance of acceptance.

> **T.M. MURPHY**   Agents and editors receive hundreds of submissions, and they are looking for every excuse not to read your manuscript. Don't give them one!

> **KRIS NERI**   Like many writers, I've found it efficient to send out a stack of queries at the same time, and I've developed an assembly-line approach. And because I never have enough time, I'm usually rushed and tired when I work on them. But I've learned to always take a few extra minutes to check the details. Have I spelled the agent's or editor's name correctly? Have I failed to change the address when I changed the name of the addressee? Are the details of the letter correct, or did those details pertain to the prior letter? Have I put the right letter into the right envelope?

A few moments of extra attention can catch those little slips. This can make the difference between a professional presentation and one that is simply wasted because it looks sloppy.

> **JOAN JOHNSON** Before submitting your manuscript, learn the mechanics of how to start a new chapter (halfway down the page), put in a header (Johnston—Chapter 1 on the left, page number on the right), margins (1 inch at the top and bottom, 1½ inches on the left, and 1¼ inches on the right). Always doublespace! Only print on one side of the page. Never bind the manuscript—use rubber bands. Cover page should have your name, address, and phone number on the upper left-hand corner (or your name, with your agent's name, address, and phone number, if you have an agent), the title centered halfway down the page, with your name three spaces below that.

You can copyright a work simply by putting your name, the copyright sign (©), and the year on the cover.

Don't worry about someone stealing your manuscript. But if you're concerned, send your manuscript to yourself certified mail, return receipt. When you get it back, *don't open it.* Just keep it under the bed. If someone later questions whether/when you wrote your book, you'll have your sealed manuscript with a postmark date to use to prove when you wrote it.

73. Developing a Track Record

No one can make you feel inferior without your consent.
—Eleanor Roosevelt

An old farmer, nervous that his son just sits around doing nothing except waiting for life to happen, looks at him and says, "Son, there are two ways to get to the top of an oak tree. You can climb it or sit on an acorn and wait."

When I first started writing seriously more than ten years ago, I knew that I wanted to be a novelist, but I also knew that to get an agent or editor interested in my work, I would have to have some kind of publishing record. Aside from a few articles I published in college, law school, and the local paper, I really had none. I had to get off the acorn and start climbing the tree.

I began writing short story after short story. This would be the route to publication, I convinced myself. But I ran into a couple of problems: The short story market was limited and so were my stories. Then I did some research in the library and discovered a small mystery magazine that published mystery poetry. I dashed home and wrote a poem about Lizzie Borden in about ten minutes and sent it off to the magazine with a self-addressed, stamped envelope. About two weeks later, I received a letter of acceptance and a $5 bill! My first royalty! Although it was only $5, something changed that day. Somebody actually thought highly enough of my work to publish it, and to pay me for it as well. And because the magazine only bought first rights, I was able to publish the poem in two other mystery journals.

That one poem gave me a track record. After that, I could write agents, editors, and short story outlets and let them know that my work had appeared in other respectable journals. As a result, my confidence increased, and I began getting acceptances for short stories and essays. I was getting paid. Not a huge wad, but that helped make me a believer.

Be clever as to how you do your apprenticeship. Find a way to build a publishing track record and keep building on it whenever you can.

> **ROBERT J. RANDISI** If you're just starting out, try writing short stories first. Even if you don't sell them it's like a rehearsal.

> **MICHAEL WIECEK**   Sadly, the best way to get published is by being famous for some other reason, as any week's nonfiction bestseller list will suggest. But if you can't manage that, the standard approach is to start small and work up—from zines few people have heard of, to more established nonpaying markets, to small-press anthos, to magazines, and to finally a book contract. At every stage, the credits are only to convince the next editor to read a few pages. That's all you can hope for. And if the writing's good, that's all you need.

Once you make a sale or two, it's worth building a reputation as a reliable and professional writer. Meet your deadlines, be polite (and charming and funny if you can manage), don't complain, and never badmouth anyone. It's a small world.

> **T.J. PERKINS**   The first thing to do to increase your chances of being published is to write a bio and create a list of your publishing credits. I decided to build publishing credits by writing Star Wars Fan Fiction, and I began getting short stories published for free through webzines. I immediately started to build a fan base.

> **KRIS NERI**   Nothing beats short story publications for building credits. But other avenues are also great. Volunteer to write a column for your local or national writing organization's newsletter.

When I first started writing, I offered to write a member spotlight column for my local Sisters in Crime chapter. That provided an on-going writing credit that I was able to include in my query, and it also allowed me to network with the published chapter members and to garner writing tips from them.

You can also write book reviews or other book-related pieces for fan publications or e-zines. The editors of those publications desperately need material. While they rarely pay for their pieces, you build writing credits and garner writing experience as well.

74. Accepting Criticism

If I were to try to read, much less answer, all the attacks made on me, this shop might as well be closed for any other business.
—Abraham Lincoln

Nobody likes a critic, but a writer should. Or at least a writer should be open to criticism. When readers criticize your work in its infancy stage, don't take offense. They are trying to help. Listen to their comments and be objective about them. All you have to do is listen. You do not have to take anyone's advice. This is your novel and chances are good that you have an idea of where you are going with this story and character. But because you are human and could be wrong, be open-minded when it comes to criticism. Some of it will be bad and some of it good. In the end, you will decide.

› **CYNTHIA RIGGS** Don't take criticism personally. Mark the passage in question, then a day or so later go over it with a fresh outlook. Either change it in accordance with the criticism, ignore the criticism entirely, or recognize that the passage was not clear and rewrite it.

Don't defend your work. If you find yourself saying, "What I meant was . . ." rewrite the passage to say what you meant.

› **KRIS NERI** No writer likes criticism. When we present our work, we hope our readers, editors, and critique partners will all rave about how perfect it is. But that's neither realistic, nor helpful if the book does have problems.

A little time always helps me to deal effectively with criticism. When I receive an editorial letter, I simply allow it to simmer on the back burner of my mind for a few days. If I try to process it immediately, I end up feeling too defensive, but a bit of time takes away the initial sting.

Within a few days, the truth always seems to sort itself out. By that point, the remarks that I know to be wrong become clear to me, along with the reasons why I don't agree with that advice, which gives me the ammunition to dispute it with my editor. At the same time, the criticisms that are true also become clear, as well as the ways to fix them.

This system almost always works for me, and it's rare these days for me to feel angry about criticism. But I've learned by now that when I do, it's because I know the criticism is true— but that I really don't want to make that particular change. But you know what they say about your darlings: For the good of the work, they have to go. At this point in my career, I understand that anger is a signal I've become too protective of something that doesn't benefit my book.

> **T.M. MURPHY** Criticism can be a wonderful gift for a writer. You're almost there, but sometimes it's that suggestion or nudge to "think of trying this . . ." from your editor that will help you up that hill to find the story you are meant to write. Be open!

75. Trusting Your Instincts

You are something new in this world. Be glad of it. Make the most of what nature gave you. In the last analysis, all art is autobiographical. You can sing only what you are. You can paint only what you are. You must be what your experiences, your environment, and your heredity have made you. For better or for worse, you must cultivate your own little garden. For better or for worse, you must play your own little instrument in the orchestra of life.
—Dale Carnegie

You can get all the feedback in the world for your novel, but in the end, it will be you who signs your name to it, and you will be the one handling publicity, asking people to buy copies, or seeking reviews. Prior to publication, you will be the one who decides what stays in and what gets edited, what direction the plot will take, what this character or that character will do or not do, etc.

At some point, if you ever want your manuscript read by an agent or editor, you will have to trust your instincts as to how your story is going to be told. But before your manuscript makes the rounds, you can educate your instincts. While your work should be original, educate yourself on what works in your chosen genre. Ask yourself why you like a particular book and what you think works well and what doesn't. What did this author do or not do. How will your story be different or better. Instincts are good to have, but like opinions, try to back them up with knowledge and experience.

> **JOHNNY D. BOGGS** My wife reads each chapter and edits them, offering suggestions, correcting mistakes, and telling me when I'm a complete idiot. Sometimes more often than not, I follow her advice. Other times, I stick to my original thoughts.

When I get to a snag, I try not to think, but react. Bottom line is: It's your story, with your name on it. More often than not, I trust my instincts. Of course, sometimes my instincts turn out to be dead wrong. And I've seldom, if ever, won an argument with my editor.

> **CINDA WILLIAMS CHIMA** You can't always trust your instincts. If you think what you just wrote is brilliant, it probably isn't. If you think you can get away with something, you probably can't. You need to know your characters well enough so that when an editor requests a change that doesn't work, you can say with perfect confidence, "No. She wouldn't do that."

76. Saving Everything

He is a benefactor of mankind who contracts the great rules of life into short sentences, that may be easily impressed on the memory, and so recur habitually to the mind.—Samuel Johnson

One of America's major American writers, George V. Higgins, author of *The Friends of Eddie Coyle*, died quite young. When I read his obituary, I was devastated to learn about his death and also to learn that by 1970, he had written as much as fourteen unpublished novels. According to his longtime friend and colleague, Boston University professor Jon Klarfeld, Higgins "dumped" the manuscripts. As a fan of Higgins's work, I was shocked to read this news. Had Higgins actually thrown away fourteen unpublished manuscripts before the success of *Coyle*? I hope that when Higgins told Professor Klarfeld that he "dumped" the manuscripts, he simply meant that he put them aside, but I have not heard of them since, and I fear the worst, as I think most Higgins fans do.

Do not throw away your work. Save everything. Especially your early material. In your early work are the seeds of your fledgling voice, your characters, your story lines. These works are measuring tools and moreover, while you may have to face the fact that a certain manuscript is unworkable as a whole, portions of it may be salvaged with great promise. Think of that wonderful character you created, that fascinating scene, or that incredible setting that just poured from your subconscious. If you throw it away, it can never be recovered. As Ben Franklin said, "Waste not, want not."

Also, the idea you came up with today may not be useful for your present project, but for one you will work on years down the road. Fortunately, when it comes time to take on this future project, you will have your ideas at your fingertips. Don't let a good idea get away.

> **MICHAEL BRACKEN**   Don't let manuscripts wither away in a filing cabinet. Keep them circulating until they sell. I wrote a short story in 1975 that didn't find a home until 2005.

> **KIT EHRMAN**   Save everything that you write, not just fiction. I occasionally write journal entries, mainly description, most about the weather, because weather figures predominantly in my series. If I'm working on a book that takes place in the dead of winter, but I'm writing it in July, it's nice to be able to flip through saved journal descriptions of snow flurries and wind chill that I wrote in January.

All this saving leads to an astonishing pile of documents, so it became critical to name documents carefully so I could find them later. My nephew, Zach, needed to save an English paper on my computer because his machine was having technical difficulties. When we went back to retrieve it a week later, he watched in fascination as I scrolled and scrolled and scrolled through my documents before I came to his, which I'd named Zach's somethingorother.

The moral of this story: Don't destroy your work. You may need it later.

> **STEPHANIE KAY BENDEL**   I have two examples to share on this subject. The first concerns a short story I wrote years ago. I called it "No One Ever Listens," and it was about a little girl with a big imagination. When she sees her neighbor burying a large bundle in his backyard and learns that his wife is gone, she tries to convince her parents—and then the police—that the woman is buried next door. But because she is only a little girl, no one listens to her. As she keeps trying to gather evidence, she arouses the suspicions of the neighbor, who comes after her. Though she manages to save herself rather ingeniously, the first editor I sent the story to labeled it "unpublishable." "No one

wants to read a story in which a young child is in mortal danger," she said. When a second editor replied in almost the same words, I realized I had violated some sort of taboo, and I threw the manuscript into a desk drawer.

About five years later, (the average amount of time that elapses between my desk drawer cleanings), I came across the story again and decided I still liked it. One of the magazines I had originally sent it to now had a different editor, so I submitted it again, and it sold. Happily, the story was shortly thereafter reprinted in an anthology for young adults. It was also reprinted in a German magazine, where it was noticed by a German filmmaker who subsequently purchased the film rights! Perhaps every story has its proper time.

The second example I want to share concerns a novel that just wouldn't come together for some reason. A few years after I'd given up on it, I chanced upon the manuscript and reread it. I still couldn't figure out how to make the novel work, but I realized that one of the subplots could become a short story in itself. I called it "The Bones in the Well," and it sold to the first editor I sent it to. Interestingly, someone else liked that story so much he changed the title and a dozen words and published it in a collection of short stories under his name! I sued for plagiarism and received even more money than I'd gotten for the original publication!

Part IV

THE BUSINESS

When you have completed your novel, it's time to switch gears from creative writing to creative marketing. This section is designed to give you an understanding of how to structure a query letter, how to work with agents and editors, and among many other things, how to build your reputation. It can be difficult for the artist in us to accept that publishing is a business, but it's true. In Tip 88, "Learning About Publishing," Michael Bracken sums things up very well when he reminds us: "Writing is an art. Publishing is a business."

If your goal is to get your novel on the shelf of major bookstores, or better yet, have readers pull it from shelf and buy it, then learn, as Mr. Bracken advises, to separate art and business. Once you do, the road to publication will be a lot smoother.

Chapter 9

NETWORKS

77. Learning from Other Writers

No one is wise enough by himself.—Titus Maccius Plautus

Early on in your writing career, you may have joined a writer's group to share ideas and motivation. Now that you're farther along in the process, however, you may want to reassess your needs, or if you haven't yet joined a group, reconsider it.

One of the best ways to become a recognized member of the genre you wish to write in is to join a writers' organization that represents your chosen genre. By becoming a member of such an organization, you immediately create an association with some of the most successful writers in your genre. Moreover, you will learn about open anthologies, which invite you to submit your work. In newsletters you will learn about what agents and editors are looking for, what's hot, what's not. You will also have the opportunity to network with fellow authors, established and aspiring. You will be impressed by the camaraderie between authors, and you will learn that your fellow writers are your colleagues, and they really do want you to succeed.

Here's an example. One night at the close of a monthly meeting for the New England Chapter of the Mystery Writers of America, one of my favorite mystery writers, multi-Shamus Award–winning author Jeremiah Healy, distributed a brochure that he had put together, chockfull of excellent, hands-on advice to aid the aspiring author's quest for publication.

Additionally, many of these organizations host functions where you can meet agents and editors who are specifically looking for manuscripts in your field.

Also, your membership is also a way for you to support your genre and to help galvanize its standing in literature.

Research the Internet for the organization that might serve you best. Chances are, no matter what country you live in, there will be a welcoming organization for aspiring writers of romance, Westerns, fantasy, crime, science fiction, and horror.

Finally, never forget how much you can learn from the writers you meet not just by talking with them, but by reading their work. This is their greatest gift to you, and when you have read their work, you will be able to broaden your discussions with them.

> **ROBERT J. RANDISI** Attend conventions to meet other writers, both new and established. Just listening to other writers converse—not speaking on stage or on a panel—can be helpful.

> **T.M. MURPHY** Some writers are no fun and no help. I have, however, had some of the best times in this business being on panels where I've met and learned from people such as the late-great Philip R. Craig (The J.W. Jackson Mystery Series), Claire Cook (*Must Love Dogs*), Tom Sawyer (writer for *Murder, She Wrote*), Jan Brogan (*Yesterday's Fatal*), and Peter Tolan (cocreator, executive producer, and director of *Rescue Me* and screenwriter for several movies). You can always learn something from hearing other writers talk shop in a real, unpretentious way.

78. Shopping for an Agent

Be nice to people on your way up because you'll meet them on your way down.—Wilson Mizner

A new writer once told me that when she received a rejection letter from an agent, she responded with a rejection letter of her own. I never heard of this writer publishing anything, and I'm not surprised. Her reprisal was a waste of time and perhaps a waste of career.

One thing I always stress with my students at Boston College is to be professional *always*. Send thank you letters to agents and editors who take the time to consider your work, even if it has been rejected. This is a small business, and kindness and good will carries the day.

When you're looking for an agent, it is very important to educate yourself on what type of market a particular agent prefers to represent. For example, if you write romance novels and submit your manuscript to an agent who only represents science fiction novels, you have wasted your time and money. You will in all probability receive a rejection that will break your heart.

› **KAT MARTIN** Agents are extremely important. They do what you cannot—tell your publisher how great you are! Agents are difficult to find, and sometimes they don't grow with you and so you have to change. Still, they are necessary to the business of writing.

› **MARY REED MCCALL** The story of how I acquired literary representation is humorous in that it highlights my naïveté at the time, but it also shows that there's nothing wrong with targeting specific agencies or agents, based upon the kind of writing you do, and then following through in a professional, courteous manner.

Back in 1994, I was a brand-new writer attending my first national writing conference, which happened to be in New York City. Panels of publishing professionals from various houses were present at the event. At that time, I was very interested in Bantam Books, because many of the authors I was actively reading then were published by that house. And so it was that after attending the "Spotlight On" session for Bantam, I mustered my courage and approached the long table of their representatives.

Only a few of the Bantam editors lagged behind because everyone—attendees and presenters alike—usually made a dash for the doors once a workshop ended. But I was undaunted. I knew that the editor I was approaching made active acquisitions of manuscripts for Bantam Books. She was a senior editor, I believe, and therefore virtually a goddess in my unschooled perspective of the publishing industry at that time.

Not realizing it was likely a strange question to pose face-to-face with someone in that position, I politely waited until she made eye contact with me. Then I asked her if she would be willing to recommend any agents with whom she and the other editors at Bantam liked to work.

She looked at me for a long moment, apparently startled by my forthrightness. Then she studied me more pointedly, as if she was trying to determine why I was asking her for that kind of information. Thankfully, she must have deemed me harmless, because with a half smile, she turned, grabbed a piece of hotel letterhead that was on the table, jotted down half a dozen names and agencies for me, and then handed it over without a word. I stumbled a little in murmuring my thanks and went away with my heart pounding from the after-effects of nerves and utter jubilation. I'd just gotten the equivalent of an "insider Habit"! I felt like I'd been given a treasure (and I had).

I'd heard of some of the agents on that list, and I proceeded to submit my work to those who seemed most likely to represent writers in my subgenre. Several of them rejected the work I had to show, but one of the agents (who was from what I'd learned was a major and well-respected agency in New York City) wrote such a helpful and detailed rejection letter that I was moved to answer with more than my usual, brief, "Thank you for having considered my work" note in response. I wrote her an actual letter, and in it I made sure to let her know how much I appreciated the time and effort she had put into giving me the feedback she had in her rejection.

More than a year later, I attended another writing conference—this one near Boston—and the agent with whom I'd corresponded was in attendance. Because it was a much smaller, regional conference, I thought it wouldn't be too forward to step up and introduce myself, to thank her once again, in person this time, for the insights she had provided. I had barely finished saying my name when she glanced down at my name badge, and her eyes lit up. She grabbed my hand and said something to the effect of, "Oh, of course I know who you are! Your name is etched into my mind because you wrote the nicest thank you letter anyone ever sent me! Consider this an open invitation to send anything you're working on in the future. No need to query first."

I was stunned, humbled, and delighted. To think that good, old-fashioned courtesy (the kind my parents had always stressed as so important in life and business) had opened this kind of door for me was wonderful and overwhelming. It took another year before I had a new manuscript to show her, and it wasn't long after that the agency offered me representation. The manuscript sold less than eight months later, to a major New York publishing house, and I am still represented by that same, fabulous agency and agent today. It was a happy ending all around, and it was achieved through a combination of old-fashioned sleuthing and good manners.

79. Writing a Query Letter

Beauty of style and harmony and grace and good rhythm depend on simplicity.—Plato

A query letter is a letter you write to an agent (or editor) requesting that he read your manuscript. You should know that each agent has different requirements as to how they wish you to draft a query, and these requirements can generally be found in writer's books or on the agency's website. Learn the requirements and follow them exactly. Nothing annoys agents more than writers who don't follow the rules.

I heard an agent speak at a writer's conference, and he said that he received on average 140 e-mails per day. That's more than 50,000 e-mails a year. Time constraints here are obvious, so you must keep your query letter simple and to the point. By knowing what must be in a query letter, you can do it like a pro. In fact, you will have to do it like a pro if you want your work considered by an agent. Here's a start.

As a general rule, in your first paragraph your query letter should state who you are and the title of the work you are requesting the agent read. If you were referred to the agent, let the agent know this in your first paragraph also.

In your second paragraph, in two or three sentences, give a powerful, exciting description of your novel and introduce the central characters. This is without a doubt the most important section of your query letter. It is your pitch. Here you are trying to sell your story, and agents want stories they can sell. That's how they make their living, so make sure your pitch whets their appetite.

In your third paragraph, state your publishing accomplishments and qualifications. If you have never published anything before, emphasize your special qualifications to write this book, such as your job and other life experiences.

In your closing paragraph, thank the agent for his time and consideration and let him know that you have included a self-addressed, stamped envelope (SASE) for his response. Without a SASE, it is likely that your submission will be shredded. Harsh but true.

Remember that agents receive thousands of submissions each year, so keep you query letter to one page. The content of the letter must be powerful and designed to sell, but keep the format simple because for an agent, time is of the essence. And yes, time is money.

) TOM SAWYER The best advice I can offer on this is by way of an anecdote. While speaking at a writer's conference, shortly before needing to compose my first-ever query letter—and somewhat daunted/mystified by the prospect, I was touted onto Susan Page's book: *The Shortest Distance Between You and a Published Book*. I spent a day and a half carefully following her paragraph-by-paragraph matrix, polishing, rewriting and punching-up, and late on a Sunday evening I faxed my initial query to an agent in Manhattan. The next morning at 7:30, I got a phone call from the agent asking me to send my pages.

By the way, for a subsequent nonfiction effort, I found Page's layout for a book proposal to be every bit as effective and on the money.

) MICHAEL WIECEK Honestly, how hard should this be? Describe your project, mention your credits if you have any, and politely ask for their consideration. Avoid passive tense, keep it under 300 words, skip the blurbs, try not to start every sentence with "I." Every guidebook out there will tell you how to format it. Just follow the rules.

And yet . . . the temptation to try to stand out, to make a unique mark, to be *cute*, is apparently overwhelming. Resist. Do you think your tone is wryly ironic? Amusingly self-mocking? Knowingly world-weary? Uh-oh. Time to start over.

Unless, of course, you really *are* capable of wry irony, wit, ennui. In which case, you're a better writer than me, your letter will effortlessly reflect that fact, and your agent will soon be calling with news of a five-house auction. For the rest of us, polite and businesslike is the way to go.

80. Working with Your Agent

Time waits for no one.—The Rolling Stones

If you seek a mass audience, you must first get an agent. An agent's main objective is to find projects they believe their editorial contacts will want to publish and stand behind.

Next to having a superlative story, one of the next best ways to attract an agent's attention is to let her know that you respect her time. Agents receive literally thousands of submissions every year, and it is nearly impossible for them to critique every submission that is forwarded to them. You can do some things, however, to give yourself a better chance at getting a full and objective read from an agent.

First, and most important, follow the agent's submission guidelines precisely. Submission requirements vary from agency to agency. If a particular agency asks simply for a one-page query letter and one-page synopsis, don't send your first chapter as well because you think it is so great. It might be, but the agent will likely throw your submission away because she will assume you are not a professional author, that you don't know how to follow rules, or even worse, that you didn't even bother to research their agency's guidelines. This might seem harsh, but consider it from the agent's point of view. She has an office to run, rent to pay, staff to oversee, and she only gets paid on commission, so she has to screen queries as quickly as possible to determine what might make her the money she needs to keep her agency going.

Second, keep your query letter to one page and make it reader friendly. Make sure all your contact information is on the material you send, and make sure that you enclose a self-addressed, stamped envelope for the agent's reply. If you don't, the agent will not likely reply.

With e-mail becoming a more and more acceptable way of communication, it is always a good idea to invite the agent to reply by e-mail if it is more convenient for her, but still enclose a SASE. And always, always, always, thank an agent for her time and consideration for looking at your work.

Generally an agency will tell you how long it will take to respond to a query. If they say four to six weeks, you will have to wait this length of time. If they don't respond by this time, it is permissible to call the agency to inquire about the status of your submission. Remember, always be courteous and professional because this may be a great opportunity for you to do a little networking with the agent or a staff member who can see to it that your work lands on the agent's desk or makes it to the top of the pile.

Another way to let an agent know that you respect her time is not to engage in multiple submissions. Many agents will ask that if you submit your work to them for consideration that you forgo sending it to another agency to give them time to review your work. If you have room in your query letter, let the agent know that they are presently the only agency considering your story. The agent will appreciate this, and even if she doesn't accept your work, she may respond quicker and hence give you the opportunity to submit your work elsewhere.

Ultimately, there is no guarantee what an agent will do with your work once it arrives, or if she will do anything with it at all. But what you are trying to do at this stage is to gain every edge you can by trying to put yourself in the agent's shoes and seeing things from her perspective. But in the end remember, your agent's purpose is to try and sell your book for the best price possible.

> **LINDA SANDIFER** Don't be afraid to ask your agent "dumb" questions. He or she believes you're clueless anyway.

> **JOAN JOHNSTON** An agent is your employee, which is sometimes a difficult concept to understand, when it seems to be the agents who are "accepting" or "rejecting" the writer. Nevertheless, don't depend on your agent to set the course of your career. He or she can advise you, but you should be the captain of your own ship. You should have some idea what you're worth and tell your agent what you expect in terms of an advance, how many books you want in the contract, etc.

Agents aren't lawyers. To protect yourself, you should understand the terms of the publishing contract that are most likely to cause you trouble: the option clause, the pay-out clause, the reversion clause, and the agency clause.

The option clause: The option clause gives the publisher the "option" to buy "your next book." That language, "your next book," is too broad. It should be limited to "your next category length contemporary romance." (Or whatever kind of book you're writing.) That way, if it takes the publisher a long time to get your book published, and you're sitting around waiting to write another book, you could write a "historical western" for a different publisher. If your publisher has the right to publish "your next book"—whatever it is—you're stuck!

Also, be sure you can submit your option "synopsis" within thirty to forty-five days of delivery and acceptance of the final manuscript. Watch to make sure the publisher doesn't say the option "synopsis" can't be submitted until thirty to forty-five days after publication of the final book. That can take up to twenty-four months, with the language of some contracts, which leaves you up the creek and unable to write for anyone else for up to two years.

The pay-out clause: Be sure that your pay-out comes as quickly as you can get it. Some publishers pay "on signing," "on delivery," and "on publication." It's the "on publication" payment that can be delayed by the length of time the publisher has to publish. (Try to limit that to twelve or eighteen months, instead of twenty-four. I had a publisher who waited twenty-two months after the book was accepted to publish!) You could end up waiting a year and a half to two years for that check. Try having the final payment made "six months after delivery and acceptance of the manuscript." That gives the publisher more incentive to get the book published so they can get their money back.

The reversion clause: There's a lot of discussion by the Authors Guild right now about an author's right to have his rights reverted when a book is "out of print." With electronic publishing, this is a nebulous area. Discuss this with your agent, who can give you the latest word on how to limit the publisher's rights to books that are actually in print in realistic numbers.

The agency clause: It's sad but true. Your agent is representing you, but you need someone to represent you with your agent. Watch carefully and make sure the following clauses are *not* in the agency clause (usually around paragraph 15 of the publishing contract), where the agent's right to receive a percentage of your income is set out.

Do not give the agent an irrevocable right to represent the book for the life of the copyright.

Do not give the agent a right to represent "all options exercised" under the contract. You might want to leave an agent after this contract expires and before you exercise the "option" for your publisher to buy another book. If you leave this clause in and change agents, you might end up paying two agents!

Do not allow your agent to represent the characters in the book. If you're writing a wonderful continuing character, you can never take that character away from that agent.

If you find any of these terms in your contract with an agent or in the agency clause in the publishing contract, and the agent hasn't discussed them with you in advance (at which point you will refuse to work with that agent with those terms), simply cross out the egregious terms and initial and return the contract to the publisher. The publishing contract is between you and the publisher, not you and the agent, and agents often "sneak in" these clauses because you're trusting them to be watching out for you. It's the fox watching the henhouse, folks!

Everything is negotiable, including the rate you pay your agent. Get a literary attorney to review any contract you sign with an agent before you sign it.

81. Working with Editors

'Tis a long road knows no turning.—Sophocles

Here's an important question for aspiring writers: How do you please an editor? Editors survive at publishing houses not necessarily by choosing good books, but by choosing books that will sell. Like everyone else in the world, editors want to eat, keep their jobs, and maintain their reputations, and they have every right to.

So maybe you have written a book that grammatically and artistically puts anything on the *New York Times* bestseller list to shame, but in the end, will it sell? When writing fiction, it might be important to recall Mark Twain's formula for pleasing his readership, "Anyone can write for those who drink wine, but I write for those who drink water. And everyone drinks water."

> **HANK PHILLIPPI RYAN**   I have an editor, a pro, who sees the completed work before it goes to the publisher. I trust her talent, experience, and judgment. She's like my second set of eyes—only much wiser than mine.

> **MICHAEL WIECEK**   You know how you can really respect an editor? Make sure that everything you send her is as well-written and as polished as you can possibly manage. They all *like* editing—after all, that's what they joined the publishing world to do—but all the other responsibilities that have been added to their job description don't leave much time for it. Diamonds in the rough are fine, but a brilliant, perfectly finished marquise-cut stone is even better.

> **MARY BALOGH**   I always welcome feedback from my editor, and I am always willing to do revisions—provided I agree that they will make the book better. In my experience, editors have the great talent of spotting what makes a story or a character weak and what will solve the problem. My editor, however, does not see the book until it is finished. Most of the time she does not even know what I am writing. No one else sees the book or any part of it until after my editor has read it and commented upon it.

> **MARY REED MCCALL**   Writing requires a strong sense of personal vision, but it also helps to have a certain level of flexibility as well. Change can be difficult, and the idea of slashing a scene or paragraph you slaved over and seemingly bled onto the page can be traumatic, but there are times when it's for the greater good of the work. The trick is to cultivate an awareness

of what's nonnegotiable vs. where you can bend. If you trust your editor, agent, or critique partner, listen openly and respectfully to what they have to say and the changes they think you should make. Then sit on their suggestions for a few days, mulling and considering them, before you determine if the changes will be for the better, or rather undermine the integrity of the work as you see it.

Most of the time, after the initial burst of panic passes, I've come to see that most of what my editor has suggested is right on the money. It doesn't always make it easier to actually cut those scenes, or add that something else over there, but it's what I logically know is the best outcome for the work. Being flexible is a worthy goal, whether in relation to self-editing or receiving critique from a respected outside source. The greater the number of people you can reach through the clarity, pace, and characterization embodied in your novel, the better for the growth of your career.

› **LAWRENCE BLOCK**   Forget about figuring out what editors want, or what readers want. Who knows and who cares? Please yourself.

82. Having Mentors

When the old cock crows, the young cock learns.—Irish proverb

I read an interesting piece in the *International Women's Media Journal* concerning the importance of mentors. Not surprisingly, the essay advocates that: "Mentors—or guides—can be indispensable to moving up in your career. They play a very important role in career planning."

If you plan to have a career in writing, you should seriously consider locating a qualified mentor who is willing to help you achieve your goals. Just make sure that your mentor understands what your goals and objectives are.

The article offers some other great advice, such as how you can communicate with a mentor. "You don't necessarily have to be located in the same geographical area to have a mentoring relationship. You can talk over the phone or communicate by e-mail rather than meeting in person. What is important is that your mentor has information you need to get where you want to go, is willing to share it and is willing to use her power and prestige to help you on your journey."

Certainly all the successful writers are too busy and besides, why would they help me? you may think. The article recommends that you should consider what you can offer the mentor and to realize that you could use more than just one mentor. This way, a single mentor is not faced with having to handle all facets of your new career path. Maybe your manuscript is already in great shape. Your writer's group has given you the nod to shop it around. Maybe you just need to find a mentor who can assist you with the submission process. Or maybe you do need a mentor who can help you with your writing.

Did you ever have a teacher or professor who encouraged you to write? Look her up. She might be delighted to offer some assistance. When I was starting out as a writer, I had a question about a publishing house, so I called the Mystery Writers of America for the answers. I spoke with a friendly old gentleman, and we ended up corresponding together for many years up until his death. During our correspondence, I discovered that he was one of the most famous espionage writers of all time, Walter Wager, the author of many great works, including *Telefon*, which became a movie staring Charles Bronson.

Publishing is a tough business, but it is refreshing how other writers really do want to help you to succeed. If you need help, just ask until you get it.

> **JENNIFER BLAKE** A mentor is like a GPS. Both can point the direction, tell you the best route, and promise that others have made the trip. However, they can't choose the destination, sit behind the wheel, or make all the correct turns along the way. Nor can they guarantee that you'll like where you are when you get there—or that anyone will be there to meet you.

> **DUSTY RICHARDS** Your mother, your brother, and friends will all say how wonderful you write. Maybe you do, maybe you don't write that well, but if you can, find a professional mentor who doesn't have to please you. Through his or her efforts, you may learn how to write.

After stumbling around for a few years, I found such a man, Frank Reuter. He red-lined every page, every line, in a perfectly good manuscript. It made me sick. When Frank edited the third book for me, he said he might not have critiqued it as hard because he was so busy reading the story. That was my first sale to a major publisher. I am working on my seventy-third book now.

> **T.M. MURPHY** I think having a mentors can be extremely beneficial because they have been there so they can relate to what you're going through whether it is getting that rejection slip, having a book signing and only two people show up, or just being an ear for you as you talk about a problem you are having with a character or plot. Writing can be a lonely world, and you need to have someone that you can just call up and vent to—someone who knows that not everyday is a great day in the world of writing. Also, when you succeed, you can share it with them.

Two of my mentors are the late John McAleer, who taught me how to write a good mystery, and my dad, James F. Murphy

Jr., who took that long walk with me from the mailbox many times and said, "Never give up."

83. Becoming a Mentor Yourself

The greatest good you can do for another is not just to share your riches, but to reveal to him his own.—Benjamin Disraeli

One of my favorite movies about writing is Woody Allen's *Bullets Over Broadway* where a lower echelon mobster is forced by his boss to read play lines with a horrible actress who just happens to be the mob boss's girlfriend. The gangster rebels at first, but little by little, as he delves more into the play script, he discovers that he has a genius for storytelling. This was, of course, a comedy, and the gangster was forced to help, but I believe the message remains the same: Help others, and you will help yourself and discover things about yourself.

This book has encouraged you throughout to seek the help and advice of others because you can learn from them. But don't forget that life is a two-way street, and people will from time to time call on you for assistance also. Your schedule is busy and your time is extremely limited, but whenever possible, read and critique the material other aspiring authors ask you to. You will be helping them, and it will give you a great opportunity to critique and analyze other people's work. In the end, this will help make you a better writer and help you with overall story development. It is true that one of the best ways to learn is to teach, so teach as often as you can.

> JAMES F. MURPHY, JR.   I am a teacher, and I learn from my students. We do not live in a vacuum. Their stories remind me of mine, maybe in a different time but similar in theme and feeling.

> **T.M. MURPHY** I've been teaching kids creative writing for eleven years, and I know it has made me become a better writer. By giving suggestions, I am constantly remembering what works and what doesn't work. I also share what I am writing with my students, and I respect their feedback because they are the age of the audience I am writing for. I never want to write down to my audience, and I always have my own little group of Nielsen-rating family to say, "You might not want to go with that."

> **MICHAEL BRACKEN** Helping other writers—formally in a classroom or when leading a workshop, or informally when standing in the hallway at a convention or participating in an online forum—helps maintain my skills. When I have to think about what I do and how I do it so that I may explain it to others, I relearn the things I already know. And questions from other writers sometimes force me to consider new ideas rather than relying on the same-old same-old.

> **JOAN JOHNSTON** It wasn't until I started teaching others how to write that I began to learn about character (all those layers of the onion) and conflict (if he's a fireman, she sets fires). As I began to teach, I learned about point of view (who's telling this story, anyway?), verisimilitude (not "the church" but "the First Presbyterian Church on the corner of Vine and 8th), tag lines (he said, she said, or an action before the speech), and pacing (speed the book up with dialogue and slow it down with narrative).

> **MICHAEL WIECEK** I've never taught writing formally, but I've been in a critique group for several years. In addition, like many authors, once I had a small reputation, friends of friends seemed to find me, manuscripts in hand, which is to say I've read and commented on a wide range of unpublished material.

It can be useful to see other writers making the same sort of mistakes that I do—POV confusion is a common example—because it keeps me alert to similar problems in my own work. But over time, I've realized that more value comes from being forced to analyze and defend my own prejudices about proper writing. If I'm going to tell someone that a particular choice of words sounds wrong, or that they need about 50 percent less backstory, I need to understand why I think so. I don't have the self-discipline to analyze my opinions in a rigorous manner on my own—even though doing so can be tremendously useful—but having to explain them to someone else is just as beneficial.

84. Not Burning Your Bridges

Great is the human who has not lost his childlike heart.
—Mencius (Meng-Tse)

Some time ago I attended a writer's conference just outside of Boston. During the conference, a panel of literary agents agreed to take questions from the audience. One of the agents probably regretted doing this.

Shortly after the questions began, a would-be author rose from the audience and launched a loaded question at one agent who had obviously rejected this author's work. The agent handled herself well, but the audience could really feel the tension. The author who put the agent on the spot publicly accomplished at least two things that day. First, she told everyone in the room that she was not professional. Second, she told the other agents that her work had already been rejected.

This was not a sound business move particularly because the agents were all there to listen to authors pitch their work. This author clearly diminished her chances of landing an agent that day. And believe me, those agents will remember that author.

The writing world is a small one. If you want to be a part of it, don't *ever* become hardened by the industry and let it pollute your reputation.

› **T.M. MURPHY**   I burned a couple of bridges in my early days and realized you can't get back over those choppy writer's waters without that bridge! Sometimes you have to bite your tongue.

› **MICHAEL WIECEK**   Hey, did I ever tell you about the time at BEA when I saw this agent going—no, wait, maybe I better not repeat that. Or how about that famous writer, you know, I asked him for a blurb and you wouldn't believe it, he said— oops, I think I'll keep that one quiet too. As for my opinions about this editor or that, well, not in a million years.

Of course you want to write great stories, but second only to that, you wish to avoid giving people reasons to reject them. Poor formatting and misspelled words are such reasons; careless personal criticism is another. Editors change houses; agents and clients are always playing musical chairs; critics receive hundreds of books a month to pick from—and they all talk to each other. Furthermore, anyone, anywhere, can post stinging reviews all over the web. Or worse. Why take chances?

Two suggestions: Don't put ad hominem ridicule, however amusing, in e-mail, even to close friends. And don't drink too much at the conventions. Go write another story instead.

85. Building Your Reputation

Life is not having and getting, but a being and a becoming.
—Myrna Loy

There is an old adage that a farmer can't thin his own field. When farmers sow seed, they plant more seeds than is necessary to ensure full propagation. If more plants sprout than is necessary, the extra plants have to be thinned, or pulled out, before they choke out the most promising sprout. In other words, these sprouts have to be sacrificed for the good of the crop. It can be difficult for farmers to have to "kill" their own offspring, even though they know it's for the best.

Writers sometimes face the same dilemma farmers do. We are faced with tough choices where certain scenes we love and worked hard on just don't fit into the story. Maybe there is a character we adore, but he is superfluous and does nothing to move the story along. What if an editor or an agent or a friendly reader points this out to you, are you willing to thin your manuscript for the good of the crop? What if an editor insists? One advantage you have over the farmer is that you can save your work or character and perhaps use them in another story. But in the meantime, if you are getting good sound advice from all around you that certain material doesn't work, think about being flexible in order to make sure you don't choke out the story with excess roots.

Handling dilemmas like this one is just one of many millions of decisions that you will make in your career to build your reputation. Build your reputation carefully: e-mail by e-mail, sentence by sentence, and page by page.

> **MICHAEL BRACKEN** Be professional at all times and treat beginning writers and junior editors with the same courtesy you expect to receive. You never know when that beginning writer's career will eclipse yours or that junior editor will have her own line.

> **KIT EHRMAN** It's natural to think of "track record" only in terms of sales. But it's so much more than that. I think of track record as a compilation of many things, more like, say, my reputation. It's either built up or torn down by my dealings with

every single person in the industry, from the agent who nego-
tiates the initial book deal, through all the publishing house
employees, then out to the world to the reviewers, booksellers,
librarians, and readers. Did I meet my deadline with an error-
free manuscript? Did I thank the publicist for entering my latest title in a contest? Did I compliment the cover artist? Was
I gracious, despite the fact that the only people in the audience
were staff? Did I remember to say thank you?

I'm conscious of the fact that I'm developing a track record
with each and every person I come in contact with, either face
to face or through my work, and I want that record to be positive. The best way to achieve that is by remaining professional
and polite in all dealings and by producing the best book that
I'm capable of and passionate about. Passion can not be under-
rated or underestimated. If I'm not passionate about the book
I'm writing, how can I expect readers to feel passionate about
it? Or the bookseller? Or the reviewer? And passion ultimately
reflects in sales. When an author becomes bored with her series
or main character, it shows, and it's time to go back to the drawing board or take a break with a standalone or new series.

86. Being Courteous

A thankful heart is the parent of all virtues.—Cicero

One thing I always tell my writing students at Boston College
is to go out and purchase a packet of thank you notes. You will
need these to thank agents, editors, authors, reviewers, and anyone else who has helped you with your writing.

While writing can be a solitary business, we require the help
of others whether we want to believe this or not. Moreover, the
help we need means that some other person is going to have to
take time out of his busy schedule to help us. Thank him with

a note. Even thank the agent or editor who rejected your work. You never know when you will meet her or have the opportunity to submit your work to her again. Your thank you note will show that you are professional, easy to work with, and know how to network. Agents, editors, and publishers like writers who know how to network. Networking sells books.

And when your book gets published and reviewed, thank the reviewer. Remember, the reviewer took the time to read your book, analyze it, and then write a review. My father, Pulitzer Prize nominee, John McAleer, once told me that one reviewer he thanked was so appreciative that he wrote my father back thanking him and stating that it was the first time an author had thanked him for his work. Thereafter, my father had a friend for life, and every time my father wrote a book, that reviewer took the time to review it.

> **KIT EHRMAN** Saying "thank you" is, pure and simple, good manners; yet, so many people forget this. They forget because they are wrapped up in themselves.

I see this happen frequently in the realm of book promotion. Many authors seem, I don't know, desperate—maybe they *are* desperate—and manners are the first thing to go. The librarian does not have to invite me to speak. The bookseller does not have to set up a book signing. The radio host or features editor does not have to interview me. The reviewer has a gazillion books to review. She doesn't have to pick mine. So, when a librarian or bookseller agrees to an event, or I land an interview, I show my gratitude by saying thank you, and I always follow up with a card dropped in the mail. Snail mail, not e-mail. Even if the event didn't go as well as planned, the librarian/bookseller put time, effort, and money into promoting the event. And every time a bookseller or librarian says yes to an event, she is opening herself up to a potentially embarrassing situation if the event is a flop. The author is not the only one who's embarrassed and disappointed. So I thank her for taking a chance.

And it should go without saying: I always thank my agent or editor for the work they've done on my behalf. And I thank my readers. Without them, I wouldn't have a job.

87. Not Being Difficult to Work With

There are two ways of spreading light: to be the candle or the mirror that reflects it.—Edith Wharton

I once heard a radio interview with Roger Daltrey and Pete Townshend of The Who. The interviewer asked the two rockers about their legendary artistic feuds and if there was any truth to the notion that these feuds led to a better artistic quality. Townshend immediately said that actually the fights had done nothing but waste an incredible amount of time.

The lesson here is a simple one. Artistic differences are okay, perhaps even expected, but no one wants to work with a troublemaker. Agents and publishers want—and need—to make money. If you are difficult to work with, agents and publishers will pick up on it, and they will be reluctant to take a chance with you. Difficult people waste time and money.

You gain nothing in this business by being difficult. You have a right to respect the integrity of your art, but be open to the suggestions of others who may have more experience with the business end of this business.

> **JOAN JOHNSTON**   No one likes a bitch or a jackass. Be nice.

> **ROBERT J. RANDISI**   Save the arrogance for when you've earned it. Too many young writers attend conventions with an attitude.

› CARLY PHILLIPS Pick your battles. Don't argue with your editor and publishing house over every little thing. Choose those that matter in the long run. Otherwise play nice with others. You'll go further.

› LORI HANDELAND There's difficult and there's doormat, neither one is a good thing. Pick your battles. If you do, your editor will know when you have a complaint that it's a legitimate one. Keep records of everything so you can back up your claims if need be. Know what you're talking about. Bone up on your grammar, spelling, and composition skills. Copy editors aren't always right, but you have to be if you're going to complain about them. Always meet your deadlines, and if you can't, make sure you let everyone involved know about the delay as soon as you do. Editors aren't inhuman. They understand that life happens. They just want to be kept in the loop.

› KIT EHRMAN When *At Risk* was picked up by Poisoned Pen Press, I thought about what kind of author I wanted to be and what reputation I wanted to develop. I decided I wanted to be a "low-maintenance" author. I would stay abreast of details that enabled me to be productive and do a good job, but I would not pester, whine, complain, or ask numerous questions as if I were the only Poisoned Pen Press author on the planet. I would not need my hand held. I would get the job done and be as professional as possible, even though I wasn't always certain what that meant. I think I've succeeded. I've strived to meet all deadlines. I am polite and always say thank you. Most important of all, when things don't go my way, I keep my disappointment to myself. The world does not revolve around me. Publishers, editors, and agents do a difficult job, and they are not *the enemy* as some authors would have you believe. Be professional at all times, and you'll reap the rewards.

Chapter 10

THE PUBLISHING BUSINESS

88. Learning about Publishing

Keep thy shop, and thy shop will keep thee.—Benjamin Franklin

It seems that all new writers face the same dilemma: You can't publish a book until you publish a book. With all the rejections new writers receive, it's very easy to believe that there is no way to break into the industry. But, somehow, writers do it everyday.

Granted, it is very difficult, but if your story is good—if it's great—and you don't give up, some agent or editor will take notice of your work and give you a chance. In addition to a great story and perseverance, a little networking will also help you break in. Develop good relationships with as many authors and agents as you can, and maybe they will recommend their agent to you. And if they do, just make sure your story is in top form. You can't afford to blow a good lead. All the networking in the world will not make a bad story good. It is up to you to write a good story and get the leads that will get your foot in the door.

> REBECCA BRANDEWYNE I think it's of prime importance for aspiring writers to arm themselves with as much knowledge about publishing as they can get, as well as to determine exactly what it is they hope to achieve by actually publishing a book.

> MICHAEL WIECEK Whenever this comes up, what the folks on the publishing side are *really* saying is, "Stop whining, dammit." Yes, it is a business, and those cold-eyed, private-equity cutthroats who are buying up all the big houses honestly believe they can slash their way to 16 percent annual growth. Not fair? Of course not. Don't like it? Too bad—neither does anyone else. Buy any established author a couple of beers, and they'll tell you: It's a crummy, lousy business.

And yet . . . here we all are, hoping against hope, writing another story.

On a more practical note, once you have a book contract, learning as much as possible about the sales process can be interesting. Laydown, sell-through, reversion rights—like any specialist vocabulary, the jargon can be arcane, but it will help you understand what's going to happen and maybe prevent common miscommunications.

There's an ancient salesman's mantra about dressing well: "You look good, you feel good, you *are* good." Fairly or not, some authors are perceived to be annoyingly needy, with all sorts of unrealistic expectations. Be professional and you can overcome this bias; talk the talk and you're halfway there.

> MICHAEL BRACKEN Writing is an art. Publishing is a business. Once I learned to separate the two, to wear my "artist" hat while writing and my "businessman" hat the rest of the time, it became easier to deal with rejection, rewrite requests, and editorial changes.

There's a common misconception that writing is a solitary act, and many writers buy into this myth. Writing isn't a solitary act; it's a collaborative venture. At nearly every point in the process other people—editors, publishers, marketing directors, sales reps, and many more—impact what a writer creates and how that work gets into the hands of readers.

One of the best things a writer can do is learn the business. Understand copyright law and contract law and accepted business practices within publishing. The more I know, the less likely I am to be taken advantage of and the more likely I am to develop strong working relationships with my editors. If I understand what happens when I miss a deadline, I'm less likely to miss a deadline. If I understand what rights I've signed away in my contract, I'm less likely to pester my editors with inane questions. If I comprehend the business, I can be part of the business, not a wanna-be peering in the window.

› **MARY REED MCCALL**   One of the most eye-opening experiences of my life as an author came in the year or so before and after the publication of my first book. Throughout that time, I came to realize that there was a whole other side to writing about which I'd known very little—the business side, with its numbers game of print runs, publishing slots, stocking issues, shelf placement, and sell-through percentages. It was a bit of a shock, after having been hitherto steeped entirely in the creative side of actually producing a manuscript.

Though it's been several years since then, I know there is much about the industry I still need to learn, about mergers and trends, the effect of covers on sales, and the ever-changing tastes of the reading public, among other things. Being adaptable and open to acquiring and assimilating all the information that comes along the way is not only necessary but also vital to having a long and healthy writing career.

89. Promoting Yourself

The supreme happiness of life is the conviction that we are loved.—Victor Hugo

Today, more and more publishing houses rely on authors to do their own publicity. This means that once you get your first book contract, only a small part of your work is done because if you don't have encouraging sales with your first book, it may be more difficult to get a contract for your second book than your first.

More often than not, it will be up to you to obtain book reviews, convince local bookstores to carry your book, and schedule book signings. Once you have a signing scheduled, you are now faced with the challenge of getting prospective buyers to show up. This is no time for modesty. Shout it from the rooftops that you are having a signing. Tell friends, relatives, e-mail contacts, the local papers, and anyone else who will listen. If you have a successful signing, bookstores will want you back.

Before your signing, make absolutely sure that the bookstore will have your book in stock well before the date of the signing. Believe it or not, the stories of authors showing up to do signings where the bookstore doesn't have their book in stock are legion. This happened to me at one of my first signings. When I told one of my colleagues on the Boston Authors Club what happened, she looked at me and said, "Well, now you really know what it's like to be an author."

A promotional thing that I do is create my own "new book release." On this release, I include my name and e-mail address and the book's title, ISBN number, price, publisher's name and contact information, purchasing locations, a very brief synopsis (this is where my pitch synopsis comes in handy), and any advance praise I have for the book.

Your new book release needs to be reader friendly and contain all the information a book dealer or prospective buyer will need to get ahold of your book or you for interviews. I like to keep my new book releases to one page because bookstore owners and managers are extremely busy and have literally thousands of requests to carry books.

Even with all your promotional efforts, you may want to consider hiring a professional publicist, who can get you book reviews, radio time, and maybe even TV time. Shop around for a reputable outfit and seek referrals from reliable sources, such as your author friends, agent, or publisher. Hiring a publicist will cost you some money, but writing is a business and you may want to invest in it like a business.

When thinking about promoting your books, the thing to keep in mind is that publishers are most happy when sales are being made. So keep asking yourself, "How can I make more sales?"

› **LORI HANDELAND**   It's difficult, maybe closer to impossible, to know what, if anything, works in promoting your book. So do what you can, what you feel comfortable with, and what you can afford. If you don't like speaking in front of groups, don't. If you don't mind sending out 2,000 newsletters, knock yourself out. If you have the cash, hire a professional publicist. They have the contacts, knowledge, and resources. Spend *your* time writing better and better books.

› **ELOISA JAMES**   Unpublished authors dream of getting a magical call from an editor, but the aftermath is frightening. All of a sudden, you're being warned that without effective promotion on your part, your book will be unnoticed by readers and stripped practically overnight. Do not quail! If you learned how to write, you can learn how to promote.

Promotion forces authors to think of their careers in terms of its future: not just the book at hand. Reinvest in yourself because that's a way of asserting that you have a future as a writer. You are not a one-book wonder!

› **T.M. MURPHY** Your book is just one of several books being promoted by your publisher. They'll do their standard press release, but they are not coming at it with your passion. You sat down and wrote this book. This is your baby. Why are you going to rely on them to tell the world to buy it? Take the ball and run with it. Call radio stations, bookstores, libraries, anyone who wants to know about your book, and the people who don't!

You have to constantly promote yourself. Here's one example. My friend Rick, who's in a local band called Earthbound Misfits, was going to play at a bar so I got the word out for him. In return, he agreed to mention me to the crowd that I was having a book signing the next week. Everyone won. I got a bunch of people to the show, and a bunch of the people from the show showed up at my book signing.

Here's another example of promoting yourself. Once a landscaper accused me of being cocky because I was wearing a baseball hat that read "Belltown Mystery Series." I told him it was no different from his T-shirt that had his landscaping company on it. Getting published and staying published is a business.

Shortly after that encounter, wearing that hat paid off. I was at Fenway Park and a kid asked me if I was T.M. Murphy. It turned out he was a fan, and his mom was head of the school's P.T.O. For several years after, I gave assemblies at the school. Don't ever be afraid to promote yourself!

› **ROBERT GOLDSBOROUGH** Every author ought to be willing to do as many appearances as possible. Being a published writer is an honor and a privilege, and all of us should be willing to vigorously promote our work. I remember hearing one author say that "I write the books. It's up to my publisher to sell them, not me." Hogwash! Promotion is not a dirty word. If writers aren't committed enough to their work to help the publisher in the sales process, they shouldn't be in the business. And publishing is very much a business. Each of us ought to be ready to attend (and even set up) signings, appear on panels and at book fairs, give talks at libraries and civic groups, and be part of writing workshops. We all need to meet the reading public (our audience, after all), and we need to help other writers, including those who are just getting started.

› **T.J. PERKINS** The Internet gives you lots of opportunities to sell yourself and your book. Get to know people, network, and join online writing groups such as Sisters in Crime or Crime Space (if you're a mystery author). I also have my website through Authors Den, which is also a great place to meet people and find out information. With so many people online, and with so many different backgrounds, jobs, people they know, etc., there's no telling what, or who, someone may know to get you a step closer to your goal.

90. Seeking Online Reviews

I have yet to find the man, however exalted his station, who did not do better work and put forth greater effort under a spirit of approval than under a spirit of criticism.—Charles Schwab

I think every writer wants to imagine that her book just received rave reviews on the front page of the *New York Times* Book Review, or Booklist, or Publisher' Weekly, but while we will always strive for such reviews, we must also be realists. The odds are against it. So what do we do? We set a review strategy into action.

One strategy is to start combing the Internet for quality online reviewers that review books in your particular genre. Go to a bookstore or the library and look at the backs of books also. More and more publishers are recognizing the endorsements from respected online reviewers. One of the best things about online reviews is that they reach the worldwide market instantaneously, thus giving your work international attention. Keep reaching for the *Times*, but in the meantime, don't undervalue or overlook online reviews. They have worldwide significance.

> **T.J. PERKINS** Bookstores want to see reviews. Schools and libraries want to see reviews. It seems that everyone wants to read someone else's opinion about your book before taking a chance on it. So do a search of people and places that would be willing to give you a review. Most are free, asking only for the book for free (of course). Then, if you have a website, make sure you have links to sites that have posted reviews of your book. One great website is *www.Page1Lit.com*. This is the only website I know that asks for a small fee, but the rewards are outstanding.

> **T.M. MURPHY** This is a lesson I have learned a little late in my career. I have received hundreds of letters from teachers, parents, and kids who have loved my books. It's a great feeling getting those letters, but when I wrote back, I should've asked them to write an online review. After all, in this world of Google, that's where people are now going. Learn from my mistake.

91. Creating a Website

There is only one thing in the world worse than being talked about, and that is not being talked about.—Oscar Wilde

Today an author must have a website if he intends to achieve competitive sales. On your site, you can advertise to the world who you are and offer information about your books and where to buy them. You can also update people on your book signing events. Make your website fun, informative, and easy to browse. For ideas, visit the websites of bestselling authors.

Also, because your website may be the public's first view of you and your work, make it look professional. You want readers to know that your work is worth the investment.

> **ELOISA JAMES** A website is an author's most valuable promotion tool, and possibly the only thing you should do. These days a website is your face to the public and your way to manage your fan base. Paper items become dated, but a website is fluid and supports your entire backlist. It's worth the investment. The bestseller lists measure *rapidity* of sales. One way you can influence those lists is by building a reader list through your website, and then telling your fans to go out and buy your new book.

Putting money in a website doesn't mean that you have to go to the best designer in the business right off the bat, but if you're doing your own website, you need to take time to learn the basic concepts of web page flow and design. You'll also need to pay for a name domain.

If you do have more money to play with, treat yourself like a small business: designate a certain percentage of your profits for reinvestment and hire a top-notch website designer.

I run a huge website (*www.eloisajames.com*). One thing I've discovered over the years is that as pages, and books, proliferate, your best bet is to hire a website *company*. One person may do a wonderful design, but will he or she update it? Go around the web and find websites you like. Get referrals from friends using website companies. You're looking for a clean, crisp design with easily navigated pages and lots of interesting, new content.

This last point is crucial. Websites need material about yourself, your books, and the world you created. And the material has to be constantly refreshed. The key is to lure readers into returning to your website over and over. There's a crucial rule of advertising: People have to see a name as many as seven times before they remember it. You want a curious reader to be intrigued by your website and return—allowing you to market your current, and also your future, books to her.

Scoot around the web and check out all the value-added content contained on sites. Some authors post newsletters on relevant historical events. Others have special pages devoted to special interest buffs who might stumble on the site and decide to try the books. Start out fairly small, with a kind of extra content you know you can easily generate.

My preference is for content related to my books—so I offer "extra" chapters to books, a peek back into a published book. I have special Readers' Pages that are only available to readers who are signed up for my mailing list. Those pages offer free short stories and crosswords made out of clues from my books.

Interactive fora, such as blogs and bulletin boards, are very popular website additions. But remember that your primary goal is to write books, not spend most of the day interacting with Internet-savvy readers. A bulletin board can be much easier in terms of your time spent, but don't get into that until you have an active fan base. There's nothing sadder than a dead BB.

Another popular aspect of a website is a contest. The contest can force contestants to read your teaser, hopefully leading to sales and, if they came to your site because they already know you, to add their names to your mailing list. Either way, a contest is a good investment! Authors vary in the contest prize. Bookstore certificates and items with value tend to attract attention of contest addicts. Some authors give away signed cover-flats, chocolate, or small presents tied to a theme in the book.

A top-flight website can cost thousands of dollars to design and run, although with that level of website you're also getting invaluable marketing expertise. Mine is expensive. I argue it's worth every penny, but you can put up a website for considerably less.

› **KIT EHRMAN**   Today, an author's website is her electronic business card. Unless you're already a big-name author, many industry professionals and readers won't take you seriously if you don't have one.

That said, the website needs to be well designed, well organized, and professional looking. An amateurish website will leave the visitor wondering if that quality translates to the writing.

Once a potential contact or customer finds my website, it can be a wonderful tool, but I need to get them there first. Doing that means mastering website page titles and keywords and making sure my pages have strong content. If a person already knows who I am, they should have no difficulty finding my website. For those who've never heard of me, I'll probably have to reach them some other way, via appearances, reviews, or interviews. If they're interested enough to look up my website, they should find what they want: quick, easily accessible information that gives them a solid impression of who I am and what my series is about.

Quality review quotes are of primary importance, followed by excerpts. As a consumer, I like to get an impression of the author's style before I buy, and I figure most readers feel the same. Graphics are great on a website, adding visual interest and aesthetics, but I don't let them take over because they're a drain on the website's load time.

Two new-ish elements of web presence include blogs and book trailers. Blogs are great if you consistently produce entertaining content and don't mind sacrificing the time and energy that goes into writing them. Book trailers can kill you if they're poorly done, but they can also be a lot of fun. The nice thing is that they only need to be created once, unlike a blog that needs to be tended to on a daily basis.

A website is a worldwide, instant access, 24/7 media kit. Keep it up-to-date and make sure the quality does your writing and your reputation justice.

92. Venturing into Online Publishing Markets

The Internet is the Viagra of big business.—Jack Welch

In the early twentieth century, authors such as Perry Mason creator Erle Stanley Gardner and Sam Spade creator Dashiell Hammett did their writing apprenticeships in the old "pulp" fiction magazines, so-called because the magazine's paper, made from bits of paper, was so cheap it was as fragile as pulp.

Pulp writers were frowned upon for writing in such a mass market medium, but for many aspiring authors it accomplished two major goals. First, it paid. Second, these cheap magazines provided a platform for their stories and therefore a potential readership. Unfortunately, there is no pulp market today for the new writer, but there is a wonderful new outlet for aspiring authors to display their works: the Internet.

If we all had our druthers, we would have our work displayed in traditional paper form; however, the Internet does offer some advantages. Online "zines," as they are sometimes called, exist for every genre you can think of. If your work is accepted, when it is displayed, it is there for the entire world to see. This is a terrific way to get your name known in your chosen genre, and in other genres as well. Even though Erle Stanley Gardner did eventually break away from the pulps, he literally had to publish millions of words before doing so. The Internet gives you the potential to reach a worldwide audience instantaneously. We all want to see our novels on bookstore shelves, but keep in mind that cyberspace just may help make that dream a reality.

› **MICHAEL WIECEK**   The advantages to publishing online are easily stated, starting with volume. There are many, many outlets for your work. It tends to be easy to submit because you don't have to bother with postage, envelopes, and paper. Response times are often quick. And once you're published, you can link to the story directly from your own website, which your fans will appreciate.

The disadvantages to publishing online are also easily stated. It's true that there are many markets, but there are also small numbers of actual readers. The quality can be uneven; prestige, elusive. And don't forget compensation—or rather, go ahead and forget it, because the majority of markets pay little or nothing. At least with small-circulation magazines, you get the tangible satisfaction of a contributor's copy.

Less commonly noted is the fact that many online markets seek only the briefest of stories. It's no accident that the rise of the Internet has coincided with the resurgence of flash fiction, short-shorts, and the like. Whatever you call them, word counts are well under a thousand. Someday a viable e-book will emerge, making it as easy to read online text as a printed page—probably within a few years, in fact—but until then readers seem to have limited patience for longer works.

There's nothing wrong with flash fiction. My shortest published story has only 275 words. But it's not good training for longer fiction. With 5,000 or 6,000 words, you learn both economy *and* character development, not to mention plotting. If you hope someday to write a good book, longer narratives make for the best practice, but you won't place many of them online.

Of course there are exceptions. Respectable pieces of considerable length are being published on the web; some markets pay a living wage; a number of authors successfully use the full panoply of online content delivery—podcasts, cell phone-downloadable texts, you name it. And who knows what the future holds? Not me, certainly. Readers will still read, whatever the delivery platform may become.

93. Knowing the Pros and Cons of Self-Publishing

Alas! The fearful Unbelief is unbelief in yourself.—Thomas Carlyle

Self-publishing your novel, or vanity publishing as it is sometimes called, is considered by many to be taboo. But many authors, including Mark Twain and Henry David Thoreau, paid to have some of their work published.

Here's one benefit to self-publishing. Having your novel in book form gives you the opportunity to display your work, do readings, seek reviews, and hopefully, develop a following that will lead you to a traditional publishing house.

If you self-publish, research the outfit you wish to publish with. You will likely need to hire an experienced and trusted editor to make sure that your book is in perfect order. Self-publishing houses may not have the team of quality editors working on books that traditional houses do.

Additionally, many new books today are published "print on demand" or "POD" as it is sometimes called, by small publishing houses. If you have a difficult time selling your novel to a traditional publishing house, a POD house is something you may also want to consider.

The way POD works is that the book is only printed when it is ordered. For example, if a book is ordered online or from a bookstore, the printer is notified by the dealer and the book is then printed and shipped. This is a great advantage to the publisher because they avoid having to take the chance of printing a large run of books that may not sell or even get distributed. And the advantage to the author is obvious. This is an opportunity to publish a book and see what the world thinks of your work.

There are some considerations, however, that you will need to make before you decide to sign with a POD publisher.

You will want to know what type of distribution they will have: Will bookstores be able to order your book and will the major online book dealers carry your book? How much will the POD publisher be charging for your book? If it is too expensive, this could easily decrease sales. Additionally, you want to know how much of a discount the publisher will give the bookstore. A bookstore's shelf space is always at a premium, so they want to sell the books that will make them the most profit. They generally look for a 40 to 50 percent discount from publishers to justify shelf space for a book. Some POD publishers offer as little as 20 percent off to bookstores, which makes carrying POD books less desirable for the dealer.

> **❯ REBECCA BRANDEWYNE** The days of muses and ivory towers, of spending years honing one's craft and suffering for one's art, belong to bygone eras. While traditional publishing has been slow to keep up with technology, newer forms of publishing have led to burgeoning print-on-demand, subsidiary, and e-book publishers on the cutting edge of that same technology and the future. All this has made it possible for anyone to publish a book. Whether that book will prove successful, however, is a different story entirely.

> **❯ ROBERT J. RANDISI** I don't think young writers should be looking for "shortcuts," such as self-publishing. I think for anyone who wants a career as a writer, self-publishing is the wrong way to go. Don't get discouraged by rejections and go the self-publishing route. Having enough disposable income to publish your own book does not make you a writer.

> MICHAEL WIECEK   Vanity publication does not count as a writing credit. I'm not going to hash out the arguments again, here—you know what I'm talking about. If there isn't a competitive acquisition process, a real editor, and a producer other than yourself taking pride in the final publication, then it's not worth the effort. Not only will the "credit" count for nothing, it will actually work against you in many editors' minds.

> T.J. PERKINS   As a new author, no one ever told me what the "proper" way to get my book published was, or even what the step-by-step process was. So, I invented my path as my actions opened the next door of opportunity. I wouldn't wish the same struggle on anyone else, so I offer insight. It's been a long, hard path for me, but it's finally paying off.

I've been writing for thirteen years. I spent the first eight years writing short stories and books. In those years, a few of my short stories had gotten published, but the books were turned down by fifty to eighty publishers.

At the time, I didn't know there were different types of publishers; I just thought all of them, no matter what they were called, were traditional publishers. However, being an author of mystery books for tweens, I targeted only those publishers that wanted mystery/children's stories, but I was still turned down. As many of you may completely understand, it was frustrating and enough to make anyone want to give up.

Then I thought that perhaps I had to go outside the lines, be completely unorthodox in my approach, and shake things up a bit.

My first book, *Wound Too Tight*, was accepted by a publisher in 2001. I was so excited. It wasn't until the book came out, and I tried to set up book signings and appearances in places such as Barnes & Noble that I learned my publisher was a print on demand (POD) publisher. I had no idea what that was or why it made my book undesirable to stores. POD means they only print the amount of books a bookseller wants; they're not returnable. If they don't sell once in your store, tough. This is why big stores such as Barnes & Noble, Waldenbooks, Borders, Books A Million, etc., won't buy nor carry POD books.

The only way around this is to contact independent booksellers—small bookstores run by small business owners. Try popping into local stores, bringing copies of your book, flyers, and business cards. I found that getting bookmarkers made at a small local printing company is great. You can make your own business cards with a template.

Tell the store owners about your book and ask if they'll be willing to have you in for a signing, but you'll have to do a consignment with the store. Of course you'll have to buy your own books from the POD publisher at whatever discount they offer. Depending on how many books you sell at your signings will also depend on how much of a profit you received from the bookstore.

Another good attack plan is to go to as many book fairs as possible, once again, buying your own books and taking them to your table. Make sure you have a tablecloth that will fit your book's theme. A slab of material from a fabrics store works great. Bring flyers with information about your book, purchasing information, your website address, etc. Keep business cards and bookmarkers handy to give away. You could also have a bowl of candy. You could raffle off a book, too. Buy the raffle tickets from a large party store.

Also keep in mind that many Barnes & Noble stores have special local author events and Educator Appreciation Nights. These are perfect events to get your foot in the door.

The whole idea when getting started is to make yourself known. Here I am, here's my book, this is what it's about, etc.

Now that you have a schedule getting full it's time to tell everyone about it. You can places ads in local papers listing your events. If ads are too expensive, try to get interviews with local medias and within those articles about you and your book try to have them list your signings.

At book fairs and signings, put a guest book on your table and encourage people to give you their names and addresses. Now you have a mailing list and can mail out your list of signings. Contact radio stations and try to get on morning shows to let people know all about you, your book, where you'll be, and when.

After doing this for four years, the public was showing me that they truly loved my books, and kids wanted more. But I felt totally trapped and held back by the POD publisher I was under. I had to take matters into my own hands.

I broke ties with the POD publisher. Once I gained complete control, I thought up a publisher name, contacted Bowker and bought a block of 10 ISBNs, found myself an illustrator and cover designer, formatted the insides of all of my books in Microsoft Word, and contacted a printer. (I chose Lightning Source. They're considered a POD printer, but if you code your books in their system as "returnable," any store can buy them. Not only that, they're linked to Ingram and Baker Taylor. All it takes is for one store, just one store, to place an order as a "back order" or "special" in their ordering system to get the ball rolling. As you get sales, Lightning Source will send you a check per month.)

I finally had all of my tweens mystery books at a lower price, they had new cover designs and illustrations, and more important, they were returnable.

How far are *you* willing to go to push a great story? First and foremost, I strongly recommend you try getting your book published through a traditional publishing house. I also strongly recommend you get an agent. Keep trying for several years before taking the hardest path. But once you start down that path, be prepared to persevere and hold fast to your belief in that wonderful story you wrote.

Chapter 11

YOUR READERS

94. Targeting Your Readers

Never forget that the reader of fiction reads to feel. He doesn't read to think and most certainly doesn't read to be bored.
—Maren Elwood

How do you know if your writing is good or not? This is a difficult question, and even if your friends and trusted critics read your work, you won't necessarily get the answer. It is not unusual to discover that your readers will enjoy parts that you don't and be leery of parts that you do like. When you have heard all the comments, however, be honest with yourself. When you wrote this section were you a bit bored too? Too much description here? Maybe this character wouldn't do this sort of thing and therefore, it is out of character. Or maybe you prolonged a scene simply because you enjoyed it or perhaps because you wanted to use some technical research that now seems shoehorned into the book. Can you edit it out now since it's no longer pertinent? You might have to make some hard cuts here that wrench your writing soul, but that scene you loved so much, might have to go.

It's fun to write what you like, but ultimately, if you want your books to sell you must please your readers.

> **CYNTHIA RIGGS**   Respect your reader's intelligence. Don't tell them everything all at once. Let them discover bit by bit what's going on. No need to lay out the entire setting, plot, and characters in the first few pages. Often you'll find your story doesn't begin until page five or even later. The first few pages were a warmup for you, the writer.

> **ROBERT J. RANDISI**   Don't write for a perceived market. It will change before you have time to finish. Keep writing what you know, what you like, what you're good at.

> **PATRICIA BRIGGS**   But if you want to get published, it is important to keep your audience in mind as well. Here's how to do this.

1. Decide who your audience is. I like to imagine my readers coming home tired from work and hoping for something to keep them entertained. This means that I don't work them too hard, because they are already tired.

2. Lead your readers through your story. Hold their hands through transitions and viewpoint shifts. This means, make it clear when you have a scene change or when the story is being told by a new person. Avoid confusing your reader if at all possible.

3. Remember that there is an agreement between a reader and a writer when the reader picks up your story. They trust you to entertain them, to make them feel, and to make them think. They trust you not to abuse them. I always keep in mind that if I kill off or abuse a major character (and I've been doing my job as a storyteller and the reader actually cares about my characters) then the reader will, when they are reading, feel just as if someone they know is being abused or dying. That doesn't mean

I don't do it—just that I'm very careful not to do it unless it is important to the story.

95. Not Underestimating Your Readers

What I mean by the Muse is that unimpeded clearness of the intuitive powers, which a perfectly truthful adherence to every admonition of the higher instincts would bring to a finely organized human being. . . . Should these facilities have free play, I believe they will open new, deeper and purer sources of joyous inspiration than have yet refreshed the earth.—Margaret Fuller

As my dear Aunt Alice used to say, "No one likes a show off." Okay, so you know the science behind how a plane actually stays up in the air, but do you really have to spend fifty pages telling the reader about it? It's great that you know these technical facts, but if it's not relevant to the story, then don't burden the reader with stuff they don't need to know. And don't burden them with superfluous explanations. They can figure out life on their own. What the reader wants to know—what the reader cares about—is how the hell the marshal is going to save the stagecoach before it's too late.

› **MICHAEL WIECEK** One rule for myself is "always under-explain." It's easy to forget how smart readers can be. Every implication does not have to be spelled out; every technology does not need to be described; nine-tenths of your background research should stay there, in the back of your head. Respect your readers, and they'll respect you.

Someone once told me, "I didn't really understand everything that happened in the last half of the book, but I couldn't stop reading anyway." Mission accomplished.

96. Not Boring Your Readers

Mediocre writers borrow; great writers steal.—T.S. Eliot

We know that writing is a subjective business, so how can we avoid being dull? Everyone's taste is different—to a degree. Perhaps the best way to avoid being dull is to learn what works in your genre and then try to make it your own. What are readers enjoying and why are they enjoying it? Learn from the masters in your field. You can do what they are doing without being called a "watered-down so-and-so." You can still create your own characters, setting, and plot, but you can employ the literary devices the masters use in order to make their stories appeal to a mass-market audience.

It is also true that if you are boring yourself in a scene, then you are most assuredly going to bore the reader. Learn about tension and conflict and ask yourself over and over again whether or not a particular scene serves the story. Stay focused on the story and what makes it interesting. Ask yourself what made it interesting enough to you in the first place to make you want to write it.

› **GREGORY MCDONALD** If you find yourself bored, then stop. If you're bored, you're boring the reader as well.

› **JOHNNY D. BOGGS** Writing's subjective. What's Shakespeare to someone could be slop to another. You can't please everyone. Readers have different tastes. That's part of the game. I just hope I entertain more readers than I bore to tears.

› **TOM SAWYER** Think of the typical TV viewer. He's sitting there in his undershirt, tired after another day at a job he despises, with a beer in one hand and the remote in the other. And if I bore him for one second, he's going to click to another channel. Similarly, no matter what we're writing, fiction or non-fiction, no matter how serious or intellectual, lightweight or modest, our target reader, vetting our work against such a standard *should* be near the top of our self-critiquing list. As Alfred Hitchcock so perceptively and *entertainingly* opined, "Drama is real life, with the dull parts left out." Write that one on your forehead.

97. Writing for Yourself

When you get used to being disappointed, the recovery time gets shorter, the time you need before you get back to work gets shorter and shorter.—Colson Whitehead

When I was in my twenties, I used to work on a farm and I was issued a knife to trim the vegetables. One day I had to tell my boss that I had lost my knife. He looked at me and said, "You know why you lost it?" He answered for me. "Because you didn't pay for it." He was right. If I had paid for that knife, it would have been mine and I would have had a greater appreciation for it. I think this same philosophy holds true when it comes to writing. When you write for yourself, what you have written is truly yours. Bought and paid for by your life's unique joys and troubles. Your words, not manufactured for the buck. And when you have a greater appreciation for your creations, your readers will know it.

› **PATRICIA BRIGGS**   We all really write the story for ourselves first. If I can't entertain myself, then I'm certainly not going to entertain anyone else!

› **BEVERLY BARTON**   Most really good writers don't write for their readers; they write for themselves. This isn't to say they don't want to please their readers, but they know that in order to write a good book, it has to be one that they love. Write the book you love and it will find an audience. If you're lucky enough to enjoy writing what's currently popular, then that's all the better for you. If you try to write whatever happens to be the latest "hot trend" and actually hate that type of book, your writing will suffer, the book will not be your best work, and your reader will sense that your heart was not in your writing.

› **JOAN JOHNSTON**   My biggest struggle as a novelist is to put my own story on paper—not to be influenced by what I think my editor, my publisher, my friends, or the reader wants to see on the page. I need to get those other people out of my writing space and focus on writing *my* story. If it resonates for me, it will resonate for my readers.

Chapter 12

THE FUTURE

98. Not Taking It Too Seriously

On the human chessboard, all moves are possible.—Miriam Schiff

I like the story about the father who sees his five sons arguing, so he instructs them each to collect a stick and bring them to him. When they do, he takes one stick and easily breaks it in half in front of them. "See how easy it is to break one stick," he tells them. Then he puts the remaining four sticks together and tries to break them and he can't. "See," he now tells them, "when you stick together, you can't be broken."

A writer's life can very easily consume every facet of your life. Don't let it. There is still a world out there and you are part of it. Your kids still need help with their homework, your dog still needs to be walked, and your spouse still needs a helping hand around the house and a hand to hold.

The world will still spin, and the day-to-day tasks will not stop at home or at work because you have decided to write a novel. In fact, these things will *help* you write a novel. Your dreams are important, and your book is important, but don't forget the important reasons why they are so. The writing business is a hard one, but that doesn't mean it can't be fun. Keep it fun as much as you can and don't take yourself too seriously. Writing a novel is important work, but don't do it at the expense of your family. Family first. There is no better ending than a happy home.

> **WILLIAM LINK**   Have fun. Writing is not brain surgery. Granted, there are times when we want to tear out our hair, or what's left of it (in my case!). If getting up every morning and contemplating the blank screen of a computer is your conception of hell, then try forestry or animal care. Writing is more a case of laser concentration than heavy-lifting.

> **LAWRENCE BLOCK**   If there's anything else other than writing that you could be happy doing, go ahead and do it.

> **MICHAEL BRACKEN**   I find it difficult to separate myself from what I do. I am a writer. I tell stories. And I can't remember ever wanting to do anything but write.

But that single-mindedness takes a toll on personal relationships. The time I spend at the keyboard is time not spent with family and friends. The difficulty of balancing writing and family was compounded early on when I had small children and a full-time job. But now that I earn my living as a freelance writer and have time for family and friends, there's no one left. I've pushed them away or blocked them out.

I can't go back and change the choices I made, but I encourage young writers to keep their lives balanced. Know when to turn the computer off. The real world is far more important than anything you can imagine.

> **MICHAEL WIECEK**   With little kids running around the house all day, it's hard enough to remember that I have a life *other* than parenting, let alone take it too seriously. It might be

different if the daily word count had some direct connection to our daily income, but you know what a writer's wage is like. I've read accounts of old-line pulp authors pounding out 20,000 words a day to earn enough to feed the family. No writer's block for them!

Maybe if I were more serious about this whole business, I'd be more successful. Hmm.

For me it's not about passion, in the sense of a deep, overriding commitment, or need, or something. I write because I enjoy having written, and because the life suits me. It's fun.

99. Trying New Things

If it goes, it goes. Don't force it.—Yiddish proverb

One of my favorite movies is *City Slickers,* staring Billy Crystal and Jack Palance. Jack Palance plays a tough old modern-day cowboy named Curly who is full of sage, the cowboy code, and home-spun advice. Curly sees that Crystal's character is a bit of a lost soul, going through a mid-life crisis, so Curly decides to share with Crystal the secret of life. He holds up his right fore-finger and says "One." And when Crystal looks confused, Curly explains, "Just do one thing at a time."

I like Curly's advice here because it reminds us to stay focused and to do one thing and do it well. Good advice from a rough-and-tumble cowboy, but it's advice we artists sometimes have to stray from. That's because it is not unusual for writers to have to step away from projects we are having trouble with to work on other projects in order to keep our creative minds at work.

Working on another project does not mean that you have to begin another novel, but if you can and want to, then do so. In the alternative, perhaps you could begin that essay you want to write, a short story, a poem, or try your hand at painting. By taking on more than one artistic project at the same time, you are continuing to nurture the creative side of your brain and this could be the very thing you need to get your novel back on track.

"One thing at a time" may be good advice in a movie, and it does play a significant role in our day-to-day obligations. When it comes to your art, however, swing open the gates and let the creative world graze until the cows come home.

> **MICHAEL BRACKEN**   Never be afraid to try new genres. I began my writing career with the intent of becoming the next great science fiction writer, yet I've found more success writing crime fiction. I never would have switched genres if a magazine editor hadn't nudged me in that direction.

> **ROBIN MOORE**   I have in many respects been an eclectic author, going from subject to subject. As a result, I have had to learn many different styles of writing from military nomenclature, to police procedure, to underworld argot, etc. It has been fun and informative, but it's not always easy, and it's very time-consuming. My advice to a new author might be to find a good vein and keep mining it for all it's worth. Stick with it.

> **KIT EHRMAN**   No matter how much I love my protagonist, Steve, no matter how eager I am to discover what trouble I can get him into next, taking a break can be immensely beneficial. I was in the middle of writing *Dead Man's Touch* when an opportunity to submit to an anthology presented itself. I didn't want to take a break, but the Sisters in Crime anthology *Derby Rotten Scoundrels* seemed tailor-made just for me. The Ohio River Valley Chapter of Sisters in Crime meets in Louisville, and when they cast around for their first anthology theme, the Kentucky Derby was a natural. Still, I was reluctant to break away. What if

I couldn't get back into Steve's voice? What if I lost my momentum? What if . . . ? All these worries. Plus, I was running out of time as both deadlines loomed.

Thanks to the chapter president's prodding, I got busy and wrote "Retribution," a procedural featuring FBI agents Ramsey and Weiler. They go undercover at Churchill Downs to thwart an evildoer's threat to infect a racehorse trainer's barn with West Nile Virus just days before the Kentucky Derby.

The break was instructive. I could write something else. I could write *someone* else. Weiler was such a different lead for me, and I came back refreshed.

Taking that break helped me then, and I have no doubt that it led to *Triple Cross* and its Churchill Downs setting. Working on another project kept me sharp and forced me to stretch.

100. Keep Writing, No Matter What

I am happier when I have something to compose, for that, after all, is my sole delight and passion.—Wolfgang Amadeus Mozart

I could offer some sage advice here, something original like: Practice makes perfect. I could offer it, but I wouldn't mean it. You don't practice writing to become a perfect writer, you practice to become better and better. To become a better storyteller. To learn structure. To create a story readers will want to visit over and over again.

There will never be the perfect novelist; however, a writer should make this her goal. Just as in any business, a writer should always try to improve and to accept always that we can make our work better. We can always improve our storylines, characterization, and dialogue. Novelists should always strive to give their readers better and better stories, and practice will help achieve this goal.

I remember when I wrote my first novel and I was advised by an author I respect enormously that most writers have to re-write their first manuscript six times before it is acceptable to submit or at least write six manuscripts. I dreaded this news of course because I had worked so hard to complete my novel and to think of it as unacceptable was, well . . . unacceptable. In the end, however, an honest assessment of my work prevailed and not only did I have to re-write my first novel six times, but I had to write at least six full manuscripts before I really felt that I had a novel ready to submit to an agent. And after my first novel was published, I learned that there were three things I needed to do desperately: practice, practice, practice.

> **CARRIE VAUGHN**   Write every day. This is how you build up the experience and stamina to be able to write many novels.

> **TOM SAWYER**   Practice, Practice, Practice. Like, every day. Or, put another way, are you a writer, or *what*?

> **RHYS BOWEN**   The best tip I was ever given was: If you want to be a writer, *write*. If you wanted to play a concerto at Carnegie Hall, you'd practice and practice, wouldn't you? But I can't tell you how many people have said, "oh, I plan to write a book some day" and yet they are not writing now. Like any craftsperson, you practice until you become comfortable in the medium.

> **MARY REED MCCALL**   If you've ever told anyone you're a writer, chances are you've had at least one or two (or several dozen) people tell you that they have a book idea too that they would love to write, if only they had the time (or some varia-tion thereof). This stems in part from the fact that most people possess at least basic writing skills, combined with the secret fan-

tasy many harbor about the imagined life of an author: sitting home in sweatpants or pajamas, blissfully pounding away at the keyboard, producing a masterpiece in a month or so, sending it off to an editor who simply can't wait to get her hands on it, cashing an obscenely large advance and/or royalty checks, and then nodding sagely when said editor breathlessly asks if you have any other ideas simmering and how soon could you have another book written?

It's a wonderful fantasy, certainly, but if it was really that easy, everyone would be doing it. Many people might possess skills in writing, yet those who would become published novelists must also possess dedication and determination. Some writers, admittedly, are better than others at the craft of stringing together words in just the right combination to produce a desired result (that others will want to read). However, what separates the "dinner party dabblers" from serious writers is the willingness to put in the work regularly, over weeks, months, and years, continuing to practice and hone their craft in order to achieve the goal of producing a completed book of which they can be proud. And that willingness to learn, to strive, to work, to be devoted to one's craft must continue, even after that first, heady publication.

Even when the ideas won't come and the blank screen or page seems almost mocking. A writer writes no matter what, calling on that driving force inside that makes him/her persist past Chapter One, Two, and Three, even when the going gets tough and the distraction of organizing closets, surfing the Net, playing a hundred games of solitaire, or undertaking mundane household chores begins to look enticing by comparison. A writer must write doggedly, consistently, and with an eye toward reaching "the end" of each project. True writing requires practice, practice, practice, and writing no matter what. There is no substitute when seeking success as a novelist.

› **JOANN ROSS** There's no shortcut to writing. Stories abound about Ray Bradbury burning his first million words because he considered them unpublishable garbage. I've never been able to document that, but I do know that in his commencement speech to the 2002 Caltech graduating class, he said, "I've written thousands of words that no one will ever see. I had to write them in order to get rid of them. But then I've written a lot of other stuff, too. So the good stuff stays, and the old stuff goes."

I'm always amused when people tell me that they plan to write a novel, once they find the time. No one believes they can pick up a cello and suddenly start playing like Yo-Yo Ma. Or that watching every episode of *Grey's Anatomy* prepares you to perform surgery. Yet, so many people seem to believe that the art of writing comes naturally.

Well, I hate to rain on anyone's happy parade, but I'm here to tell you that it doesn't. Strong prose doesn't flow out of some magic wellspring in the ground. It has to be dug out by hard work; then it takes lots and lots more work to clean it up and polish it to a publishable sheen. Writers never get to go on cruise control; we must constantly set the bar higher, improve on our craft, put our best stuff out there, then force ourselves to come up with even better stuff.

Even Picasso had to learn to draw before he could paint. He's a perfect example of the axiom that if you learn the craft, the art will follow.

The old joke about how to get to Carnegie Hall is every bit as true for writers as it is for musicians: How do you get to see your novel in a bookstore? Practice, practice, practice.

101. Continuing to Learn and Grow

I believe that one of life's greatest risks is never daring to risk.
—Oprah Winfrey

My mother died from breast cancer. She put up a long and steady fight. One of the ways she fought the disease was to read the daily newspaper in order to keep on top of current events. Two days before she died she looked up from the paper and said to me, "Did you hear the news!" She knew she was dying, yet still had a genuine excitement for news. To be a novelist you must keep learning. The next thing you learn might get you through that plot snare you've been struggling with for the past week. Or that word you picked up through the cubicle at work today . . . ? You didn't know what it meant, but when you hit the dictionary it turned out to be the very word you've been looking for since last Thursday. Then of course there is the satisfaction of knowing that someday a reader might look up from your novel and say to their child, "Did you know that the pony express only lasted from April 1860 to October 1861?"

> **CARLY PHILLIPS** Know that the learning process never ends. As a writer, you need to grow constantly or else you'll get stagnant and so will your career.

> **CARRIE VAUGHN** Always be working on the next thing. Always have the next project ready to go. By the time your first novel gets published, the second should already be finished. Also, if your first novel doesn't sell, by the time you've collected all the rejections, you'll have the second one ready to go, and it'll be better. My first novel published was the fourth I tried to sell. It was the sixth I wrote.

EPILOGUE

The weakest kind of fruit drops earliest to the ground.
—Shakespeare

Did you ever have to shuck corn? The husks aren't that bad to contend with because you can just strip them right off and bundle them up for the compost heap. But the corn silk? Well, that's another story. You pick at it and pick at it and curse it and to no avail, try to shake it off your hands. It's endless. It seems like you'll never get that ear in shape for the boiling pot.

Anyway, did you know that for each kernel of corn there is one strand of corn silk? The individual corn silk strand is like the umbilical cord for each kernel. Without it, we don't have corn. Each strand serves a purpose. If you're lucky enough to find a full, robust ear, you know that each strand of silk has done its job well. Against all odds, this tiny, future castoff has survived drenches and drought, predator and plowshare.

Your novel is not much different.

Sow your words and nurture them. Give them each a purpose and protect that purpose. Every word, sentence, paragraph, page, and chapter is fed by your thoughts, feelings, and instincts. And when you, against all odds, have completed a story that works, you know that each strand of silk has done its job and has done it well.

Finally, never stop taking take sustenance from Jane Austen's words from

Northanger Abbey: "'Only a novel' . . . in short, only some work in which the greatest powers of the mind are displayed, in which the most thorough knowledge of human nature, the happiest delineation of its varieties, the liveliest effusions of wit and humour are conveyed to the world in the best chosen language."

Everything else is just grist for the mill.

INDEX